IT'S ENOUGH TO GIVE YOU THE HUMP

HORRIBLE GEOGRAPHY

DESPERATE DESERTS

ANITA GANERI ILLUSTRATED BY MIKE PHILLIPS

SCHOLASTIC

Also available

Bloomin' Rainforests · Cracking Coasts · Earth-Shattering Earthquakes ·
Freaky Peaks · Monster Lakes · Odious Oceans · Perishing Poles ·
Raging Rivers · Stormy Weather · Violent Volcanoes · Wild Islands

Horrible Geography Handbooks
Planet in Peril
Wicked Weather
Wild Animals

Specials
Intrepid Explorers
Horrible Geography of the World

Scholastic Children's Books,
Euston House, 24 Eversholt Street,
London, NW1 1DB, UK

A division of Scholastic Ltd
London ~ New York ~ Toronto ~ Sydney ~ Auckland
Mexico City ~ New Delhi ~ Hong Kong

First published in the UK by Scholastic Ltd, 2000
This edition published by Scholastic Ltd, 2008

Text copyright © Anita Ganeri, 2000
Illustrations copyright © Mike Phillips, 2000, 2008

ISBN 978 0439 94455 7
All rights reserved

Printed in the UK by CPI Bookmarque, Croydon

10 9 8 7 6 5 4 3 2 1

CONTENTS

INTRODUCTION

Geography. What on Earth is it all about? Some geography teachers drone on and on about far-flung places you've never heard of, using lots of posh words even they can't spell. Is this what your horrible geography lessons are like?

TODAY'S LESSON IS ALL ABOUT AEOLIAN TRANSPORTATION.* WE SHALL BEGIN IN THE KYZYL KUM...**

DID WE SKIP A PAGE?

* That's the posh way of saying a blast of wind. No, not that sort of wind. The sort that whips the sand up into sand dunes in the desert.

** Kye-zul-kum. Part of the Turkestan Desert in Central Asia. See what I mean about spelling?

WHAT IS SHE GOING ON ABOUT?

DUNNO. SOUNDS LIKE GIBBERISH* TO ME

*Careful! You're beginning to sound like a geography teacher. You've accidentally used a horribly technical desert word. A gibber is a stony desert plain. You'll be setting yourself homework next.

Luckily, not all geography is as desperate as this. Some bits are positively sizzling with excitement. Take deserts, for example. Don't listen to your gibbering geography teacher. Deserts are one of the most brilliant bits of geography ever. To find out exactly how brilliant, try this simple experiment to turn your bedroom into a desert.

Go into your bedroom and put all the lights on. Then turn the heating up full. This will make your room nice and bright and hot. Almost like a real desert. Then chuck a truckload or two of sand and gravel all over the floor. Plant a nice clump of palm trees (a few of your mum's best pot plants would do). And, if you're feeling really ambitious, get down to some digging and pile up some of the sand into a soaring sand dune. Congratulations! You've got your own desperate desert. Sort of. If your grown-ups start moaning like mad, smile sweetly and say you were only doing your geography homework. Then they can't complain. (On second thoughts, ask permission first.)

HOW MUCH D'YOU THINK IT WOULD COST TO HIRE A CAMEL?

And that's what this book is all about.

Hot enough to fry an egg, dry enough to drive you mad with thirst, and full of some very prickly characters, deserts are horribly hot potatoes. In *Desperate Deserts*, you can…

• fry your brains as temperatures reach 58°C.

• see the sun blotted out by a deadly duststorm.

• find out how to get water out of a frog.

- learn how to survive in the world's driest deserts with Sandy, ace explorer, and Camilla, her faithful … camel.

This is geography like never before. But a word of warning before you read on. Go and fix yourself a good, long drink. Come to think of it, fix yourself a fridge full. Discovering the desperate deserts can be horribly thirsty work…

TO TIMBUKTU, AND BACK, TOO

France, 1824

The young man with the mop of brown hair could not believe his eyes. Surely there must be some mistake. He read his newspaper again.

WANTED

Intrepid explorer.
For expedition to Timbuktu.
Must come back ALIVE.
First prize: 10,000 francs.
Apply to the Geographical
Society of Paris.

It sent shivers down his spine.

The young man's name was René Caillié (1799–1838). He was far too skinny and frail to look like an intrepid explorer but that was precisely what he wanted to be. Never mind Paris, René wanted to see the world. One part of the world in particular. You see, for as long as René could remember, he'd dreamed of going to Timbuktu where the houses were said to be made of gold.

RENÉ CAILLIÉ | INTREPID EXPLORER

There was just one teeny problem. Tantalizing Timbuktu was in Africa. In the middle of the Sahara Desert in Africa, actually. Getting there was going to be horribly tricky.

René was born in La Rochelle, France, the son of a baker who liked to drink and ended up in prison. It wasn't a great start in life for the lad and worse was to come. What happened was this. René's father and mother died when he was young and he and his brother and sisters were brought up by his old granny. After leaving school, he went to work in a shoemaker's shop but he was always late or in trouble. His mind simply wasn't on the job. It was miles away ... in Africa! On his days off, restless René shut himself in his room, staring dreamily at the dog-eared map of Africa pinned on the wall.

How he wished that he was there. Especially in the bits of Africa mysteriously labelled "desert" or "unknown". Every spare minute was spent with his nose in a book about travel and adventure. No wonder he was late for work. René was so busy reading books that he often forgot to go to bed. (Don't try this excuse at home.)

Now his dreams might just come true. The ad in the paper seemed to be written just for him. This was an opportunity not to be missed. The Geographical Society, too, had heard rumours of Timbuktu's fabulous gold and saw a chance for some serious money-making trade. Before anyone else found out about it. There was no time to lose. René grabbed his chance of a lifetime…

Various places in Africa, 1827–28

In April 1827, René finally set off for Timbuktu. Actually, he'd arrived in Africa some years earlier, with his granny's blessing. (Anything to stop him moping around the house, she said.) But he couldn't go anywhere without money. (Any money he'd had had been spent on getting to Africa.) So he got a job in a factory and saved up all his pay. In his spare time, he learned the local desert language and got into training by walking for miles and miles each day. Everything was almost ready. There was just one small (well, large-ish) hitch. You see, Europeans weren't actually allowed into Timbuktu, only Muslims. If René was caught, chances were he'd be killed. (And that would never do. In order to claim the Geographical Society's prize, he had to make a detailed account of everything he had and done in Timbuktu.) Did this put him off? No way! He'd come this far and wasn't about to give up now. Instead, René came up with a cunning plan. He'd disguise himself … as a Muslim, wearing long, flowing robes and a long, flowing headdress so that no one could see his face!

JUST BLEND IN... JUST BLEND IN...

It was brilliant, though he said it himself! (He couldn't actually tell anyone else for fear they'd see through his disguise. Tricky!) He'd keep his notes hidden in a copy of the Qur'an, the Muslims' holy book. Then if anyone saw him reading his notes, he could always say he was praying. And in case anyone asked him why he had such a strange accent, he'd say he'd been kidnapped as a child and carted off to France. Now he was returning home to Egypt. OK, so it was a bit of a long shot.

On 19 April 1827, René finally set off with five local people, three slaves, a porter, a guide and the guide's wife. It was a dreadful journey. It was desperately hot and despite all the training René had done, his feet were torn to shreds. His path led through thick, fly-infested forests of grass, up steep mountain paths, through fast-moving streams and swampy bogs.

He lost his way three or four times a day and several times people almost saw through his disguise. But worse, much worse, was to come. In August, when he was about half-way, René fell desperately ill with a nearly fatal attack of fever. He felt rotten. And just as he was recovering from that, what happened? He collapsed with an abominable bout of scurvy, so bad that the skin peeled off his mouth. Yuck! He never could eat properly afterwards. (Note: scurvy is a horrible disease you get by not eating enough fresh fruit and veg – you have been warned!) Luckily, a kindly villager nursed him back to health with nourishing rice-water and herbs. (Sounds even worse than your school dinners.) And as soon as plucky René was better, he was back on his (still very sore) feet again. He spent the last bit of his journey travelling by canoe, down the Niger Riger, hidden under a mat so that no one would see his face.

Finally, on 20 April 1828, just as the sun was setting, brave René Caillié reached the desert and Timbuktu. At long, long last, his dreams had come true. Or had they? The books on Africa said that Timbuktu was so fabulously rich that not only were its streets paved with gold, but every house had a golden roof. Every day, it was said, caravans of camels arrived in the city, loaded down with yet more gold. Poor René had never been so bitterly disappointed in all of his miserable life. (Which just goes to show, you should never believe everything you read in books.) After everything he'd been through, the heat, the dust, the rice-water and herbs, he found himself in a city of "miserable houses made of mud", where "not even the warbling of a bird could be heard." (René's own words, not mine.) There wasn't a golden house in sight.

The Sahara Desert, Africa, 1828
But there was no time to lose feeling sorry for himself. Getting to Timbuktu wasn't enough. To get his hands on the 10,000 franc prize, he had to get back home again – ALIVE!

It was easier said than done. The only other explorer to reach Timbuktu had been savagely strangled to death by his guide. Would René live to tell the tale? It was going to be horribly tough. You see, reckless René chose to return by a different route. A route that led north, right across the desperate

Sahara Desert. It was a journey no European had ever tried before, let alone seen the end of. Things didn't start well. René very nearly missed the bus, er, camel. He had hitched a lift with a camel caravan which was going his way. But he was so busy saying goodbye to his new Timbuktu pals that his fellow travellers got fed up and left without him.

René had to run so fast to catch them up that he fainted. Luckily for him, someone picked him up and plonked him on his camel. Only another 1,600 kilometres to go...

For the next four months, René, his 400 companions, and their 1,400 camels travelled thirstily across the desperate desert sands. Woe betide anyone who fell asleep in the saddle. If you dropped off, you were left behind.

It was tough but rules were rules. The journey was worse, far worse, than anything René had suffered before. Day after

15

day, they trudged slowly across the seemingly endless sands and desolate rocky wastes. The glaring sun was terrible; the sandstorms were worse, blistering their lips and throat. The caravan was attacked by unfriendly locals. What's more, the food, if you could call it food, was absolutely foul – a mouldy mixture of flour and honey. (And to add insult to injury, René was nicknamed Camel Face because of his big nose.) But this was nothing compared to the throat-parching thirst. Camel Face, er, sorry, René, was thirsty all the time. It was like the worst type of torture. All day long, he could think of nothing but lovely, wet, dripping water. But lovely, wet, dripping water was strictly rationed to one drink a day and wells were few and far between. Many of them had run dry. Some of his companions were so desperate they bit their fingers to drink their own blood, or even drank their own urine. And when, finally, the caravan did make it to water, René had to fight off the camels to get a drink.

Eventually, utterly exhausted, burned to a crisp, with his clothes reduced to rags, René stumbled into Tangier in Morocco and went straight to the French Consul's house, expecting a warm welcome. Guess what? After all he'd been through, the Consul mistook ragged René for a beggar and kicked him out on the street. When finally he got back home to France, things began to look up for René. Not only was he given a hero's welcome, he was also awarded a medal, a generous pension and the Society's prize. But he'd had enough of exploring to last him a lifetime and gave up his travels for good. Instead he settled down and got married. And did he live happily ever after? Not quite. You see, not everyone believed his story. Some people said he'd made the whole thing up for the sake of the money. After all, he couldn't actually prove he'd been to Timbuktu. They only had his word for it. Who do you think was telling the truth?

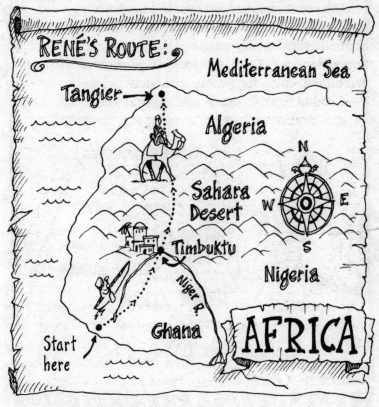

RENÉ'S ROUTE:

Mediterranean Sea

Tangier

Algeria

Sahara Desert

Timbuktu

Niger R.

Nigeria

Ghana

AFRICA

Start here

Desperate desert fact file

NAME: Sahara Desert

LOCATION: North Africa

SIZE: 9 million sq km

TEMPERATURE: Up to 45°C in the day; down to −7°C at night

RAINFALL: Less than 100 mm a year

DESERT TYPE: High Pressure (see page 28)

DESERT DATA:

• The biggest desert on Earth. It's as big as the USA (or Australia, with room to spare).

• In Arabic Sahara means desert. So you don't really need to say Sahara Desert, do you?

• About a fifth of the Sahara is covered in sand. The rest is rocky, pebbly and salty.

• About 6,000 years ago, it was green and wet with crocodiles, hippos, giraffes and elephants.

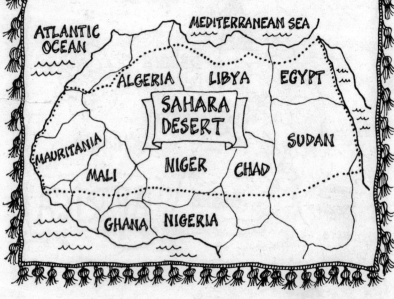

Sandy here. If you're thinking of following in René Caillié's footsteps and having your own adventure of a lifetime, you'd be in good company. Plenty of horrible geographers have had a go at exploring the desperate desert. Some of the lucky ones, like René, have even made it back alive. Could you stand the heat? Before you saddle up your camel and head off into the sunset, it might be an idea to dust up on your desperate desert know-how. (Don't worry, you'll have Camilla and me for company.) You never know, it could be a matter of life and death.

DRY AS A BONE

There might not be a desert near where you live but there's plenty of desperate desert around. In fact, deserts cover more than a third of the Earth's surface, and they're growing all the time. But what on Earth are deserts, and who on Earth gave them their desperate name? Horrible geographers can't agree (for a change). Some people blame the ancient Romans…

"DESERT" COMES FROM A LATIN WORD WHICH MEANS A DESERTED OR ABANDONED PLACE

Other people blame the ancient Egyptians…

"DESERT" COMES FROM AN EGYPTIAN WORD WHICH MEANS, GUESS WHAT? A DESERTED OR ABANDONED PLACE

Desperate, eh? Whoever thought of it first, the word desert stuck. (Thank goodness "abandoned place" didn't catch on. What a mouthful!) Though it's a mystery why the Romans had a word for a desert when they lived in the middle of

Italy. (Where there isn't a desert in sight.) The expert Egyptians, on the other hand, knew all about desperate deserts. They lived in the Sahara, which as you know, is the biggest desert on Earth. Not that they visited it very often. They thought the desert was full of demons and that anyone mad enough to go wandering off in it was likely to get their just deserts, sorry, desserts.

What on Earth are desperate deserts?

Warning – you'll need to use your imagination for this next bit. OK, here goes. Imagine you're walking along a sandy beach on a breezy day. (Put your fingers in your ears so you can't hear the sea.) It's the middle of summer and baking hot. There's no one else around. Your skin's starting to burn and your lips taste salty and dry. Your throat's so parched you can barely swallow. And when the wind blows, it flings stinging sand straight in your face. But more than anything else in the world, you're absolutely dying for a drink. Trouble is, there's nothing but sand for miles and miles. No water, no shelter, no ice-cream van. Desperate, eh? Welcome to the desert.

Hot and dry

There are two sure-fire ways of spotting that you're in a desert (if you hadn't already worked it out). Generally speaking, deserts are:

1 Baking hot

During the day, deserts can get desperately hot with temperatures well over 50°C. IN THE SHADE! (Yep, there's shade in the desert, if you can find it. Look out for a rare tree or bush, or a shady cave.) The ground's hot enough to fry an egg and toast your toes! The hottest temperature ever recorded on Earth was a sizzling 82°C in the Sahara. To get an idea of what this feels like, take the hottest summer's day you can think of. Now double it. Is that hot or what? At night, though, it's a different story. Because there aren't any clouds to trap the heat, temperatures can plummet well below freezing. Desert winters are even worse. Wrap up warm if you're planning a winter break in the Gobi Desert. You can expect teeth-chattering temperatures of −21°C and below. Brrr! Come to think of it, you'd probably be better off staying at home.

2 Bone dry

If you're off to the desert, leave your brolly behind. (On second thoughts, take it, it'll make a good sunshade.) It's extremely unlikely to rain. That's what makes a desert so desperate. Horrible geographers used to count deserts as places which got less than 250 millimetres of rain a year. That's about the height of the water you have in the bath, if you can remember where the bath is... Which sounds quite a lot but it's spread out over the whole of the desert. But now they've gone and changed their minds. (Geographers are always going and changing their minds.) Now they use a new-fangled system called an aridity index.

Aridity is the tricky technical term for dryness. But "dryness index" doesn't sound very impressive, eh? It's obviously much too tricky for some horrible geographers. They still stick to the millimetre method. Cowards!

Here's how the aridity index works. (Note: there are two different versions of this experiment. One's for a desert scientist with loads of high-tech equipment. The other's for you to try at home.)

See how dry a desert is – version 1

What a desert scientist would do:
a) Measure how much rain falls in a year in the desert (using high-tech equipment like rain gauges, radar and satellites).
b) Measure how much water evaporates (dries up) in the sun (using more high-tech equipment).
c) Divide **b)** by **a)**.

See how dry a desert is – version 2
If you can't get to a desert to do this experiment, don't worry. You can always try it at home.

What you do:
a) Count the number of cans of pop in your fridge, say two.
b) Then count how many friends you've got round who all want a drink, say eight.
c) Now, divide your friends by the number of cans to give an aridity index of four! (8 ÷ 2 = 4)

Congratulations! Your house is officially semi–desert. Count your lucky stars you don't live in the scorched Sahara. It scores an incredible TWO HUNDRED on the aridity index. Which means it loses 200 times more water than it gets. Talk about bone dry. But that's quite enough boring maths for now. Have a can of pop as a reward!

Desperate desert weather
Rain clouds? Where would we be without them? In the desperate desert, of course. Want to know why deserts are so deadly dry? It's because there aren't any rain clouds around. Sand and rocks, yes, palm trees, maybe, camels, probably. But rain clouds are extremely rare. Which, oddly enough, is what makes them so horribly important. To find out why, you first need to see how a rain cloud grows:

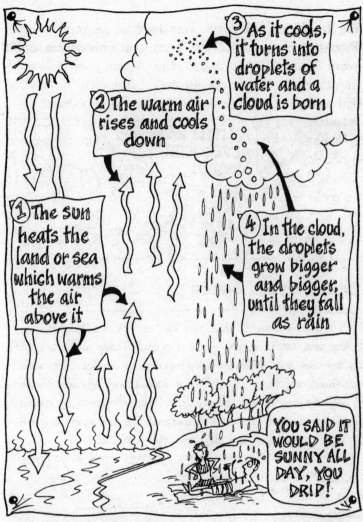

So why don't you get rainclouds in the desert? The trouble is that the warm air doesn't have a chance to cool down. It's so hot in the desert, it dries the air up. So rain droplets rarely form. Which is not to say that it never rains in the desert. Take the record-breaking Atacama Desert, for a start. Officially, it's the driest place on Earth, even horrible geographers agree about that. Some parts of the desert went without rain for 400 years (from 1570 to 1971). But desert rain is horribly unpredictable. When it finally rained, it poured, and poured, and poured, causing chaos and furious flash flooding.

Desert weather forecast

It always pays to keep an eye on the weather. Here's the sort of thing you might expect... Today will start off hot and dry, with the wind getting up in the afternoon. There may be a chance of a dust storm or two if the wind is very strong. Expect cooler temperatures by evening. Tomorrow will be much the same, and the next day, and the next day, and the next day...

You get very strong winds in the desperate desert because there's nothing to slow them down. They race over the ground, whipping up great choking clouds of dust.

And it doesn't stop there. Dust from the Sahara gets blown hundreds of kilometres, as far as the USA. Where it can fall in the rain and snow, turning them both bright red. Spooky! It must really get up people's noses. Especially as the Sahara's the dustiest desert on Earth, churning up 200 million tonnes of the stuff a year!

How on Earth do deserts happen?

Like geography teachers, desperate deserts are all horribly different. But they all have one thing in common – they're all desperately dusty and dry (a bit like geography teachers).

Any rain around simply passes them by. So how on Earth do deserts happen? Dip into Sandy's red-hot guide and find out about four different desert types.

27

Ⓐ Name: HIGH PRESSURE DESERT
Location: On either side of the equator
Aridity index: Very high
How they happen:

At the equator, warm air rises and blows away to the north and south. There the air cools down and sinks. How on Earth does this make a desert? Good question. Well, meteorologists (geographers who study the weather) call this high pressure because the sinking air pushes down on the Earth, putting the Earth under pressure. See? And high pressure brings sunny days and clear, cloudless skies. Sounds like perfect desert weather.

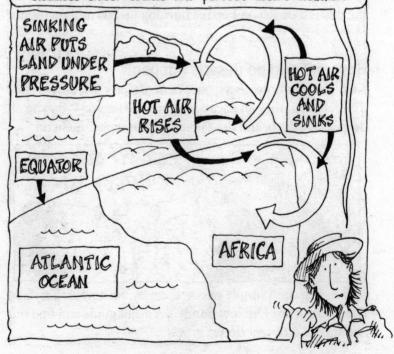

SINKING AIR PUTS LAND UNDER PRESSURE

HOT AIR RISES

HOT AIR COOLS AND SINKS

EQUATOR

AFRICA

ATLANTIC OCEAN

B Name: RAIN-SHADOW DESERT
Location: On the sheltered side of some mountain ranges

Aridity index: Very high

How they happen:

This is what happens when a mountain range gets in the air's way. As air rises up to get over the mountain tops, it cools down into droplets, and forms rain clouds. But by the time they've reached the other side of the mountains, they've dumped all their dampness as rain. So the spooky thing is that you can have desert on one side of the mountains and fabulous forest on the other.

RAIN CLOUD

RAINLESS CLOUD

MOIST AIR FROM SEA

RAIN SHADOW

DRY AIR

DESERT

© Name: INLAND DESERT
Location: In the middle of some continents
Aridity index: Very high
How they happen:

Usually, winds blowing across the sea carry masses of moisture for making rain clouds. But these inland deserts are so desperately far away from the sea, they don't stand a chance of rain. By the time the air's blown for thousands of kilometres, any clouds and rain are long, long gone.

Name: COASTAL DESERT
Location: Off the western coast of some countries
Aridity index: Very high
How they happen:

Chilly currents flowing off the coast cool the air blowing inland. So it's much too dry to create a cloud. But fit some fog lamps on your camel. In the morning, the ground's still cold. It hasn't had a chance to warm up in the sun. In turn, it cools the air above it. Then the air condenses (turns into liquid water) and forms a thick, clammy blanket of ... fog. Bet that's the last thing you'd expect to find in a desert.

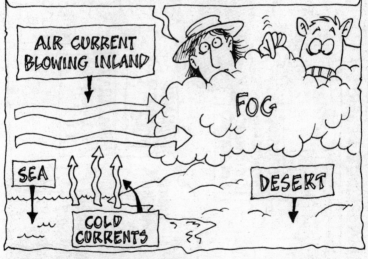

AIR CURRENT BLOWING INLAND

FOG

SEA

DESERT

COLD CURRENTS

Desperate Deserts Top Ten

Over the page there's a handy map to show where on Earth the top ten deserts are and the type of desert you might just find yourself in.

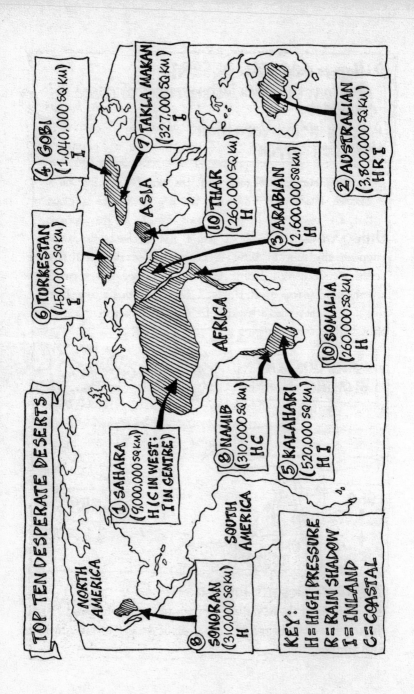

TOP TEN DESPERATE DESERTS

KEY:
H = HIGH PRESSURE
R = RAIN SHADOW
I = INLAND
C = COASTAL

① SAHARA (9,000,000 SQ KM) H (C IN WEST; I IN CENTRE)

② AUSTRALIAN (3,800,000 SQ KM) H R I

③ ARABIAN (2,600,000 SQ KM) H

④ GOBI (1,040,000 SQ KM) I

⑤ KALAHARI (520,000 SQ KM) H I

⑥ TURKESTAN (450,000 SQ KM) I

⑦ TAKLA MAKAN (327,000 SQ KM) I

⑧ NAMIB (310,000 SQ KM) H C

⑨ SONORAN (310,000 SQ KM) H

⑩ THAR (260,000 SQ KM) H

⑩ SOMALIA (260,000 SQ KM) H

NORTH AMERICA

SOUTH AMERICA

AFRICA

ASIA

32

Dying for a drink

Faced with all the things desperate deserts can throw at you – the horrible heat, the dust, the fog, it's a wonder anyone goes there at all. Or comes out alive. You need to be tough to survive in the desert. As this terrible true story shows. Picture the scene…

The Sonoran Desert, USA, August 1905
Dawn was breaking over the desert. It was going to be another desperately hot day. Scientist, William J. McGee lay fast asleep on the ground. A lizard strolled lazily across his leg and somewhere in the distance a hungry coyote howled.

William shifted slightly in his sleep but he didn't wake up. He'd been in the desert for three long months, studying desert weather and wildlife. Compared to the deadly creatures he'd seen, lizards were, well, er, pussy cats. Besides, he was having a very strange dream. In it, a herd of huge cows was galloping towards him, closer and closer, raising clouds of dust with their hooves. Suddenly, one cow let out an ear-splitting ROOAAARRR!

This time, William woke up with a start.

"What the…? Where's…? Who's the…? Mummy!" he mumbled, looking around blearily and reaching for his gun.

Of course, there wasn't a cow to be seen anywhere. Then William realized what it was he'd heard. He hadn't dreamed the scream – it was real. And whoever had made it wasn't far away. And desperately needed his help. Wide awake now, William scrambled to his feet and peered over the edge of the nearby cliffside. A dreadful sight met his eyes. A man lay on the ground. He was barely alive, his body a bag of bones. There was no time to spare. If he didn't have a drink soon, he'd die. William sloshed water over the man and gave him a sip of whiskey to drink. (Desperate times called for desperate measures.)

Then, slowly and painfully, through parched lips, the man began to tell William his story:

"My name is Pablo Valencia," he gasped. "My friend and I came to the desert to look for gold. There's an old gold mine we heard of and we wanted to make some money. We knew that summer wasn't the best time to come but we thought what the heck, we'll be OK. Anyway, somehow we got split up. My friend had our horses and supplies. I was left stranded and alone with only a canteen of water to drink. It was desperate. I tried to get back to the waterhole. I knew it must be nearby. But the heat was so terrible, it played tricks on my mind and I couldn't find the way.

At the end of the first day, my water ran out. It was terrible. I was so thirsty, I can't tell you how thirsty. It was like I was being tortured. I tried chewing on some twigs. I even ate some spiders and flies. But they just made me sick. At night, some vultures flew overhead, waiting for me to die. It seemed to go on for ever. I don't know how long it was. All I know is that soon I couldn't hear or focus my eyes. I couldn't speak or swallow. I was so weak I could hardly move. But I had to carry on. What else could I do? I crawled along for a while, but I knew that it was over. I said my prayers and I lay down to die. It was then that you heard me scream. It was one last desperate plea for help."

35

Plucky Pablo had had a lucky escape. He'd spent seven long, desperate days lost in the desert. If William hadn't found him when he did, he'd have died of thirst for sure. In fact, he went on to make a full recovery. But how on Earth did he survive for so long without water? What do you think he drank to save his life? Was it...

A) CAMEL PEE B) HIS OWN PEE C) HIS BLOOD

Answer: b) And he wasn't the first. Like many desert travellers before him, Pablo drank his own pee in a last-ditch attempt to quench his thirst. People have also tried drinking camel pee, blood (their own and their camels') and even petrol. DO NOT TRY ANY OF THESE AT HOME.

Teacher teaser

If you are dying for a drink but there's still an hour to go before lunch, try sucking up to your teacher with a spot of ancient Greek. Put your hand up and say:

PLEASE, SIR, MAY I BE EXCUSED? I'M FEELING A BIT EUDIPSIC

He'll be so gobsmacked, he's bound to let you go. But what on Earth are you talking about?

Answer: Eudipsic (you-dip-sick) is the technical word for being thirsty. If you're a serious show-off, you could always try hyperdipsic (high-per-dip-sick) for being very thirsty and polydipsic (polly-dip-sick) for being so desperately thirsty you'd drink anything (even camel pee?).

Horrible Health Warning

In the desperate desert, you can die of thirst. Literally. Without any water, you'll be dead in two days. Tops. First, you'll lose loads of water as sweat. You'll feel weak and your skin will get dry and wrinkly. Next you'll feel feverish and confused. Your blood quickly gets too thick for your heart to pump, followed swiftly by delirium and death. Nasty. To stay alive, drink at least nine litres of water a day. (That's the same as 27 cans of fizzy drink. Burp!) Even if you don't feel at all thirsty. But drink it in sips. Don't gulp it down. Otherwise you'll be horribly sick and waste the water. How can you tell if you're dehydrated? Look at the colour of your pee. It's normally a lightish yellow in colour. But if it goes darker, you're in trouble. Have something to drink immediately.

Still desperate to go? Well, you have been warned. And don't forget, if you're determined to trek through the deadly desert, take as much water with you as you can carry. You never know when you'll find the next welcoming well or waterhole. Besides, you're going to need all the refreshments you can get to help you through the next choking chapter. It's all about bone-dry sand.

SHIFTING SANDS

So far, all the deserts you've come across have been full of miles and miles of baking hot sand, with a scattering of palm trees and camels. Exactly what you'd expect a desert to look like. But deserts aren't always quite like that. In fact, only a quarter are sandy at all. (Tell that to your teacher.) Most are made up of miles of rolling, rocky plains, covered in piles of pebbles and gravel. A few have mountains in the middle. (They're all that's left of violent volcanoes. Don't worry, it's been millions of years since these freaky peaks last blew their tops.) But if it's sand you want…

Seven sizzling facts about sand

1 Never ask a horrible geographer a simple question, unless you've got plenty of time on your hands. Take "What on Earth is sand?", for example. A geography expert will waffle on and on about aeolian (ay-ow-lee-an) lowering until you fall asleep.

That's the tricky technical term for the way in which the desert wind smashes rocks into smithereens. Aeolian's ancient Greek for wind. Rather long-winded, if you ask me.

But the simple answer is that sand is made up of minuscule fragments of rock between 0.2 and 2 millimetres wide. Which is this big…

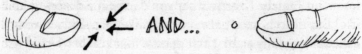

AND…

2 Sand isn't always, er, sandy coloured. Sometimes, it's black, or grey, or green. It all depends on the type of rock it's made from.

3 Some geographers have another theory for how some sandy deserts were made. According to them, the sand was spread by horrible hurricanes. It's difficult to say if they're right or wrong. After all, these hurricanes happened 18,000 years ago, and even your geography teacher can't remember that far back.

4 Strictly speaking, the superstar Sahara's the sandiest desert in the world. But that's only because it's so bloomin' big. Otherwise, the largest single stretch of sand is the Rub al Khali, or Empty Quarter, in the Arabian Desert. It covers an area of 560,000 square kilometres – about the same size as France. Fantastique. But don't expect to find shops selling ze fine French bread and cheese. It's not called empty for nothing.

5 Picture the scene. You're in the desperate desert, dreaming of slurping an ice-cold drink, when suddenly the sand bursts into song!

Yes, you heard right the first time – the sand starts singing. What does it sound like? It depends. Sometimes it's a deep, booming hum or a squeaky soprano. Geographers don't know for certain what sets the sand off. One theory is that it's because each sand grain has a coating of a shiny chemical called silica. This makes the sand grains stick together. When you step on a sand dune, you scatter the sand and the movement makes it sing. Or something. You could say it's a case of sand tunes, not sand dunes. Ahem.

Local people don't agree. "Singing?" they say. "Pah!" It's actually the sound of sinister sand-spirits laughing their socks off at stranded travellers. Or the sound of a bell coming from a monastery buried beneath the sand. Ding! Dong!

6 If you think that's weird, spare a thought for the people of Lyon, France. They woke up on 17 October 1846, to find that their city had gone … rusty!

I'VE ONLY JUST HAD THIS PAINTED

What had happened was this. Far away, in the sand-strewn Sahara, tonnes of red sand had been picked up by wind. It later fell as blood-red rain. When the rain dried, it left behind what looked like a thinish coating of rust. No wonder they were worried.

7 Sometimes the wind whips up the sand into a frenzy. Woe betide you if you're caught in a sandstorm. It can sting your skin, make you choke and even strip the paint off a car. The best thing to do is to crouch down low and cover your face and eyes.

An especially savage sandstorm hit Egypt in March 1988. Howling winds hurled tonnes of sand into the air. In Cairo alone, six people died and 250 were injured. Many others had trouble breathing.

It's hard to imagine what being stuck in a sandstorm must be like. Here's how one eyewitness – an explorer called Richard Trench – described the experience:

Teacher teaser

Desperate to get out of double geography? Why not smile weakly at your teacher and say:

PLEASE, MISS, I'M NOT FEELING VERY WELL, THE SAND'S GIVEN ME A HEADACHE!

Is there a grain of truth in what you are saying?

Answer: Amazingly, there is. At least it worked for German geographer Herr van der Esch. Sandstorms made his head throb horribly. Why? Well, during a sandstorm billions and billions of grains of sand smash into each other. This creates friction* which sends static electricity crackling through the air. And this gives some people a splitting headache. Painful.

*Friction's a force that happens when two objects try to push past each other and slow each other down. Like when you're late for a lesson and you're running down the school corridor and you bash into someone coming the other way. Or when Camilla tries to push in at a waterhole. Ouch!

Sand-astic sand dunes

Did you know that there are seas in the desert? Sandy seas, of course. Complete with sandy waves. How can that be? Well, as the wind blows across the desert, it piles the sand up into giant wave-like dunes. The biggest sand dunes stand 200 metres high (that's 20 times taller than your house) and 900 metres wide.

Imagine building a sandcastle that big on the beach. Each dune contains billions and billions of sand grains and weighs millions and millions of tonnes.

One man with a really soft spot for sand dunes was British soldier and scientist, Brigadier Ralph Bagnold (1896–1990). When he wasn't off fighting, he was studying sand. His big break came in the 1930s when he was stationed in Egypt and Libya. There he led lots of expeditions into the Sahara Desert to study the effects of wind-blown sand. Yawn! Back home in England, he built himself a wind tunnel where he could carry on his sandy studies. What do you think he found out about sand?

THE WORLD'S FINEST HANDLEBAR MOUSTACHE

a) that sand is scattered about the desert willy nilly.

b) that the wind makes set patterns in the sand.

c) that camels kick the sand up into dunes.

Answer: b) Sand dunes don't just happen by accident. The wind blows the sand into different patterns which are repeated again and again. The size and shape of sand dunes depends on the speed and direction of the wind. Brainy Bagnold set out his ideas in a book called *The Physics of Blown Sand and Desert Dunes*. Which might sound deadly boring to you but it's riveting bedtime reading for budding geographers.

Spotters' guide to sand dunes

Having trouble sorting your seifs from your barchans? Getting your transverses in a twist? Don't worry. Help is at hand. Why not sneak a look at Brigadier Bagnold's very own notebook. You'll soon be able to make sense of sand. (Note: Of course, these aren't the Brigadier's actual notebooks. They're lost in the sands of time.)

45

1 Barchan – crescent-shaped sand dunes. They form when the wind blows steadily from one direction. Here's one I made earlier in my wind tunnel:

a) The wind blows the sand along. If it meets an obstacle, like a boulder, a bush or a dead camel, the flow slows down.

b) The sand settles and starts to pile up.

c) It's blown up the side, higher and higher...

d) Until it reaches the top.

e) Then it topples and spills down the other side.

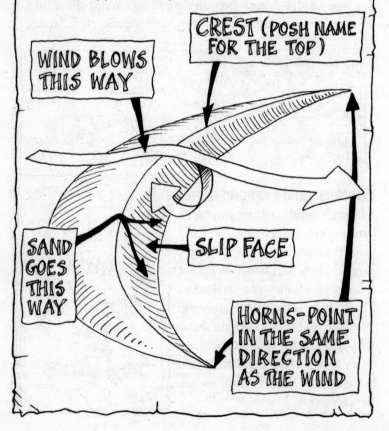

CREST (POSH NAME FOR THE TOP)

WIND BLOWS THIS WAY

SAND GOES THIS WAY

SLIP FACE

HORNS-POINT IN THE SAME DIRECTION AS THE WIND

2. Seif (sayf) – It's Arabic for sword. And sword's a very good name for these beauties because of their knife-sharp crests. They're snaky S-shaped dunes formed when the wind blows from two opposite directions. They're tall, growing up to 200 metres high, and up to 100 kilometres long.

WIND BLOWS THIS WAY

3 Transverse – Long, rounded ridges of sand, like giant sandy waves. Can be up to 300 kilometres long. They form at right angles to the wind. The valleys between them are so straight and true, you could drive a truck along them.

WIND BLOWS THIS WAY

4 Star – (My personal favourites, R.B.) They're formed when the wind keeps changing direction. And they look like giant starfish sneaking across the sand. Though if I saw a starfish this big in front of me, I'd be off like the wind...

Earth-shattering fact
Sand dunes can move. It's true! As the wind blows sand over the top, the dune creeps forward. Very shifty. Woe betide anything that gets in its way. Whole towns and villages can be buried. And these dastardly dunes are horribly fickle. They drift along dustily for years and years, then suddenly change direction. There could be one heading your way. Time to get shovelling. And it means that the desert landscape is constantly changing, which can be very disorientating for travellers.

Secrets of the sand

Apart from towns and villages, many other deep secrets lie buried beneath the desert sand. Some have been there for years. Millions of years. Are you daring enough to go dinosaur hunting?

July 1923

The Daily Globe 🌍
The Gobi Desert, Mongolia

DINO GRAVEYARD FOUND IN GOBI

Ace American explorer, Roy Chapman Andrews, was today enjoying his new-found fame.

A team of experts led by Andrews has just unearthed a batch of fossilized dinosaur eggs – the first ever known. Andrews, who cuts a dashing figure in a wide-brimmed hat complete with feather, was understandably thrilled.

"In spite of the pessimistic predictions before our start," he told our reporter, as he posed for a photograph, "we have opened a new world to science."

Dodging desert danger
He has every reason to be pleased. Very pleased. The 13 oblong-shaped eggs were found in one of the remotest parts of the Gobi Desert, a place as empty and unwelcoming as the surface of the moon. Andrews told us how the team had to travel

TICKLED PINK

49

hundreds of kilometres through the desert to reach them, braving sandstorms and bandit attacks on the way. Instead of camels, the team travelled in a fleet of converted Dodge motor cars, another expedition first.

DUNE BUGGY

Ancient egg-snatcher caught

Experts have been given the chance to examine the extraordinary eggs and believe they may have been laid some 80 million years ago. They were perfectly preserved by the bone-dry heat and soft desert sand, remaining hidden and untouched . . . until the American team found them.

SCRAMBLED EGGS

But that wasn't all Andrews discovered. More prehistoric surprises were to come. A further search revealed the bones of a small, toothless dinosaur near the nest, apparently caught red-handed as it tried to steal the eggs.

I'll be back, says Andrews

Before returning to his post at the American Museum of Natural History in New York, USA, Andrews plans to lead several more fossil-finding expeditions. "This is just the start," he said. "There may be hundreds more desert dinosaurs waiting to be discovered." And judging by what he's unearthed so far, things should get very exciting. Readers of the *Daily Globe* will be kept right up-to-date with the latest developments. With our exclusive coverage, it'll be just as if you were actually there.

RAIDERS OF THE LOST EGGS

Them dry bones

Dashing Roy C Andrews turned out to be right. There were loads more desert dinosaurs. He went on to find more dinosaur eggs and other fantastic fossils. His desert digs turned him into a star. The museum promoted him to director (not bad for someone who started out sweeping the floor) and he had a dinosaur named in his honour – *Protoceratops andrewsi*. (Why not try naming a dinosaur after your teacher?) He also wrote several bestselling books, including the gripping *In the Last Days of the Dinosaurs*.

Since then, scientists from all over the world have tried their luck in the dinosaur graveyard. And they haven't been disappointed. So far, they've dug up the bones of hundreds of dinosaurs, not to mention mammals and reptiles. The most exciting find of all was a dinosaur with feathers. It proved what scientists had thought all along – that early birds were descended from dinosaurs.

51

Desperate desert fact file

NAME: Gobi Desert

LOCATION: Central Asia (China and Mongolia)

SIZE: 1,040,000 sq km

TEMPERATURE: Hot summers up to 45°C; bitterly cold winters down to −40°C

RAINFALL: 50–100 mm a year

DESERT TYPE: Inland

DESERT DATA:

• In Mongolian, its name means "waterless place".

• It's the coldest desert in the world (apart from Antarctica).

• Most of it isn't sandy but bare rock and stones, with massive mountains on three sides.

• It's home to Bactrian camels (they're the ones with two humps).

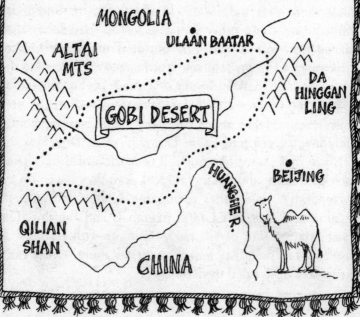

Designer deserts

Where do you find giant mushrooms and upside-down boats? And huge, stony tables? In the desperate desert, of course. They're all rocks carved into shapes by the weather.

HE TRIED TO PICK A MUSHROOM ROCK!

Over millions of years, the weather wears the desperate desert landscape away. Geographically speaking, this wearing away's called erosion. Time to check out the main earth-movers-and-shapers involved:

- Horrible heat and cold. Baking hot days and freezing cold nights have an earth-shattering effect on the desert. By day, the rocks get hot and expand. At night, they shrink in the cold. Then the whole thing starts all over again. Day after day. Eventually, all this heating and cooling takes its toll. There's an ear-piercing BAAANNGG! as the rocks split apart at the seams and shatter into pieces.

BANG!

- Rare rainfall. In the desert, it never rains but it pours. A sudden downpour can devastate the landscape. One minute it's dry as a bone, the next there's a flash flood racing towards you.

ONE MINUTE IT'S CHUCKING ROCKS AT ME, NOW IT'S TRYING TO DROWN ME!

(It's called a flash flood because it happens in a flash. Simple.) Flash floods carve out deep-sided gashes in the rocks, and sweep along tonnes of sand and boulders. When the rain stops, the water slows down and dumps its load. Then it evaporates. Just like that.

- Wild wind. Apart from stirring up sand dunes, the wind sends the grains of sand bouncing across the ground. Geographers call this saltation (which is Latin for leaping and jumping). Here's what happens:

1 The wind picks up a sand grain from the ground.

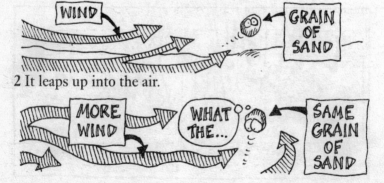

WIND

GRAIN OF SAND

2 It leaps up into the air.

MORE WIND

WHAT THE...

SAME GRAIN OF SAND

3 Then falls to the ground.

4 Then the whole thing starts again…

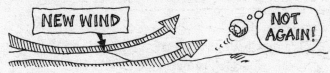

5 Sending the sand grain bouncing across the ground. Boingggg!

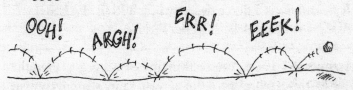

What on Earth has this got to do with erosion? Well, the wind blasts the sand at the desert rocks, wearing them away like a gigantic, and I mean gigantic, piece of sandpaper. But the sand can't bounce up very high. Instead it scrapes away at the rock close to the ground but can't reach up to the top. This goes on for years, until you're left with a rock shaped just like a mega-huge mushroom! Can you spot the difference?

Could you be a desert geomorphologist?

A geomorphologist (gee-ow-morf-ologist) is a horrible geographer who studies desert features. Well, it beats being called a boring old sand scientist. Fancy giving it a go when you leave school? (What d'you mean? You're not that desperate?) See if you've got what it takes with this quick-sand quiz.

1 An *erg* is a deadly desert disease. TRUE/FALSE
2 A *reg* is a one-humped camel. TRUE/FALSE
3 A *wadi* is a dried-up desert river. TRUE/FALSE
4 A *mesa* is a type of mountain. TRUE/FALSE
5 A *feche feche* is a fierce desert wind. TRUE/FALSE
6 A *playa* is a salty lake. TRUE/FALSE

Answers: 1 False. You're thinking of a l-erg-y. Geddit? *Erg* is the Arabic word for a vast sand sea covered in shifting sand dunes. Remember the lonely old Empty Quarter in the Arabian Desert? It's an enormous *erg*. **2** False. That's a dromedary – you're not even close! Though it's quite a cool name for a camel. *Reg* is the Arabic word for a stony, pebbly desert. It looks a bit like an old-fashioned cobbled street. **3** True. It's a deep gash or valley gouged out by a flash flood. A *wadi* can be dry for years and years, until a heavy downpour fills it with rain. Then you get a rare desert river.

"WADI'S" GOING ON HERE!

4 True. Geographically speaking, a *mesa* is a type of flat-topped mountain. It's left sticking up when the land all around it has been eroded away.

It also happens to be the Spanish word for table. But never mind knives and forks or table cloths. Some *mesas* are so enormous, you could fit a whole village on the table top. **5** False. *Feche feche* is actually very soft sand with a deceptively hard crust on top. It can measure just a few metres across or carry on for several kilometres. To be avoided at all costs, especially if you're in a car. Chances are it'll get you horribly bogged down. **6** True. Usually a *playa*'s dry as a bone but it fills up with water after heavy rain. When the water dries up in the sun, it leaves a layer of sun-baked salt behind. *Playas* are the flattest places on Earth. Flat as pancakes. Which is great news for space shuttle pilots. How? Well, one large *playa* in California, USA, is used as a landing site for the space shuttle. Cosmic.

OK. You've been walking for days and days. You've seen enough sand dunes and mushroom rocks to last you a lifetime but you haven't yet met a living thing – plant, animal or human. And you're beginning to feel a bit lonely. Desperate for company? Great news! Find out who or what is waiting to meet you as you drift over the page...

ONE HUMP OR TWO?

A desert may look deathly quiet and deserted but in geography things aren't always what they seem. Despite the horribly hostile conditions, desperate deserts are surprisingly lively and lived in. For hundreds of hardy plants and animals, deserts are home, sweet, home. So why don't they get all hot and bothered? Prepare for a sizzling surprise or two.

Keeping cool

If you despair at the thought of double geography, try spending a day in a desert. Don't fancy it? Talk about sticking your head in the sand! Luckily, there are dozens of daring creatures who call the desert home. But how on Earth do they do it? How do they cope with the heat and the drought? There are two main secrets to staying alive.

a) Finding water. All living things need water to survive. (And that includes you.) Otherwise their body bits can't function properly.

b) Staying cool. It's hot in the desert. Dead hot. Especially during the day. (That's why you don't actually see many animals. They're all fast asleep somewhere nice and cool. Zzzzzz.)

OK, so neither of these things are a problem in your geography classroom, with its leaky roof and its heating which never works. But in the desert they're a matter of life and death. Try this cool quiz to find out how some desert creatures cope.

Chill out quiz

1 What does a darkling beetle drink?
a) Rain.
b) Fog.
c) Cactus juice.

2 How does a sandgrouse fetch water for its chicks?
a) In its beak.
b) In a bucket.
c) In its feathers.

3 What does a ground squirrel use as a sunshade?
a) Its tail.

b) Its mate.

c) A camel.

4 How does the desert tortoise cool down?
a) It stays inside its shell.
b) It pees on its back legs.
c) It rubs spit on its head.

5 What does a fennec fox use its ears for?

a) Radiators.

b) Fans.

c) Er … hearing.

6 How do spadefoot toads stand the heat?

a) By living underwater.

b) By living under a cactus.

c) By sleeping underground.

7 How often do kangaroo rats have a drink?

a) Never.

b) Twice a year.

c) Once a month.

8 How do snakes cross the hot sand without getting burnt?

a) By hitching a lift on a camel.

b) By flying over the sand.

c) By slithering sideways.

Answers:

1 b) This beetle lives in the bone-dry Namib where it doesn't rain for months on end. So what does it drink if there isn't any water? Well, this ingenious insect drinks fog that rolls in off the sea. On misty nights, it stands on its head on a seaside sand dune, wiggling its back legs in the air. The fog condenses on to its body, then trickles down into its mouth. Brilliant, eh?

2 c) The sandgrouse lays its eggs in the scorching Saharan sand. The trouble is there's nothing for its thirsty chicks to drink. So the male sandgrouse flies off to an oasis and dives into the water. His feathers are specially designed to soak up water like a sponge. Back home, the chicks simply suck his feathers to get at the water. Simple. The sandgrouse is a doting dad – fetching the water often means a round trip of 100 kilometres or more.

62

3 a) The Kalahari ground squirrel uses its big, bushy tail as a parasol. It holds it over its baking body, at a jaunty angle, to give as much shade as it can.

4 b) When it gets really hot, the desert tortoise pees all over its back legs. Embarrassing but true! The pee dries in the sun and cools the toasted tortoise down.

5 a) The fennec fox uses its enormous ears to give off warmth, a bit like huge, furry radiators. Blood vessels flow across the surface of each ear, carrying warm blood with them. As air blows across them, it cools the blood (and the fox) down. Of course, the fox's ears also make brilliant, er, fox's ears, for listening out for juicy gerbils. Yum, yum!

6 c) Spadefoot toads spend nine months asleep in cool, underground burrows, lined with nice, damp slime. But at the first sign of rain, they leap into action. They hot-foot it to the nearest pool and lay their eggs in the water. Within two weeks, the eggs have hatched into tadpoles, the tadpoles have turned into frogs, and the frogs have hopped off into the desert. Then it's bedtime again.

7 a) Believe it or not, kangaroo rats never have a drink. They get all the water they need from seeds. Thirsty hawks and coyotes don't need to drink either. They simply gobble up a thirst-quenching kangaroo rat.

8 c) During the day, the acrobatic sidewinder rattlesnake has a clever way of getting across hot sand. It flips its body sideways and launches itself across the sand. In this way, its body only touches the sand for a few seconds and doesn't get burnt. Normally, though, sidewinders try to avoid the daytime heat and only get out and about at night when it's cool.

Snake, rattle and roll

Many desert snakes are poisonous. Deadly poisonous. To make matters worse, they're almost exactly the same colour as sand which makes them horribly hard to spot. Rattlesnakes have particularly poisonous reputations. But are they really as sinister as they seem? Some years ago we sent our *Daily Globe* reporter to find out more about them. And who better to ask than the world's leading expert on rattlesnakes, Laurence M Klauber (1883–1968), also known as Mr Rattlesnake. He spent 35 years studying, dissecting and writing about rattlesnakes. If he didn't know the answers no one would. Here's what he had to say.

When did you start getting interested in rattlesnakes?

When I was a boy in California. We didn't live too far from the desert, you see, where plenty of rattlesnakes live. I was really hooked on reptiles. But I was 40 years old before I started studying them seriously.

What did you do before that then?

I worked for an electrical company. I started off selling electric signs and ended up as president. I was really very lucky. But my real love was always reptiles.

So why did you leave?

I wanted to spend more time with the reptiles. So I became Curator of Reptiles at San Diego Zoo. They'd got several snakes they couldn't identify and they called me in to help. And I never left. It was a dream come true!

Do you ever take your work home?

Sure I do. I've got 35,000 rattlesnakes and assorted reptiles pickled in jars in my basement.

Gulp! And where did you get all those snakes from?

From the desert, mainly. If you're interested, a spring night's the ideal time to go. That's when the rattlesnakes are most active. Sacks are the best thing for catching them in.

Er, no, thanks, I'll give it a miss. And are rattlesnakes really deadly?

Not if you treat them nicely they're not. They'll only turn nasty if you get on their nerves. If you don't disturb them, they won't attack you. But if one starts rattling, turn around calmly and start to walk away. Whatever you do, keep your distance.

I'll take your word for it. Have you ever been bitten?

Er, yes, but only once or twice. I was lucky, it wasn't a particularly poisonous snake. The most dangerous rattlesnake is the eastern diamondback. Its markings make it tricky to spot and its bite can be fatal to humans.

Right. And what's all this about a rattle?

RATTLE!

The rattle's made up of hollow, scaly rings at the tip of the rattlesnake's tail. When the snake shakes it, it makes a buzzing sound. Sounds quite eerie, in fact. It's meant to warn enemies to leave well alone. If they don't, the snake will strike. Also, you can tell individual rattlesnakes apart by the number of rings in their rattles.

Any tips for not getting rattled?

WHERE'D SHE GO?

Yes. Wear a good pair of boots and a long pair of thick trousers, that's my advice. Then you might stand a chance. And if you're bitten, get yourself along to a doctor fast. Oh dear, are you feeling all right?

Earth-shattering fact

Forget rattlesnake-proof trousers. The deadliest creature in the desperate desert is the desert locust. Alone, these little fellows look small and harmless (one could perch happily on your thumb). But they never travel alone. These unstoppable insects fly around in swarms up to ONE THOUSAND MILLION strong. And they're horribly hungry! They devastate farmers' fields, devouring every plant in sight. What a swarm can guzzle in ONE DAY would feed 500 people for a year. Farmers have tried spraying them with super-strong insecticides but nothing seems to spoil their awesome appetites.

Design a desert-creature competition

Think you could do better? Why not enter our hot new competition to design the perfect desert animal? The fabulous first prize is an unforgettable camel safari through the record-breaking Sahara Desert. (Can I come with you?) Don't forget, you need to come up with a creature that can cope with baking heat, freezing cold, sandstorms, dust and lack of water. So it needs to be pretty special. Any ideas yet? Here's a clue — there's one desert animal that would win first prize in any creature feature competition (as long as it wasn't a beauty contest). Its survival skills are second to none. Can you guess what it is? Give in? It's the amazingly adaptable ... camel, of course. Forget cats and dogs. Camels are my favourite animals. And here's my very own Camilla to model the latest in camel cool...

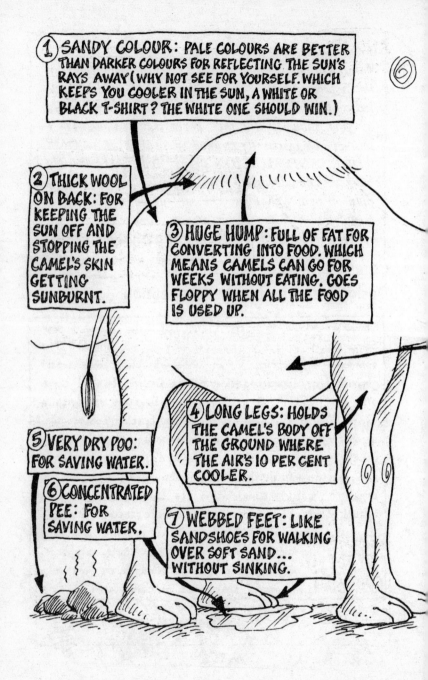

1 SANDY COLOUR: PALE COLOURS ARE BETTER THAN DARKER COLOURS FOR REFLECTING THE SUN'S RAYS AWAY (WHY NOT SEE FOR YOURSELF. WHICH KEEPS YOU COOLER IN THE SUN, A WHITE OR BLACK T-SHIRT? THE WHITE ONE SHOULD WIN.)

2 THICK WOOL ON BACK: FOR KEEPING THE SUN OFF AND STOPPING THE CAMEL'S SKIN GETTING SUNBURNT.

3 HUGE HUMP: FULL OF FAT FOR CONVERTING INTO FOOD. WHICH MEANS CAMELS CAN GO FOR WEEKS WITHOUT EATING. GOES FLOPPY WHEN ALL THE FOOD IS USED UP.

4 LONG LEGS: HOLDS THE CAMEL'S BODY OFF THE GROUND WHERE THE AIR'S 10 PER CENT COOLER.

5 VERY DRY POO: FOR SAVING WATER.

6 CONCENTRATED PEE: FOR SAVING WATER.

7 WEBBED FEET: LIKE SANDSHOES FOR WALKING OVER SOFT SAND... WITHOUT SINKING.

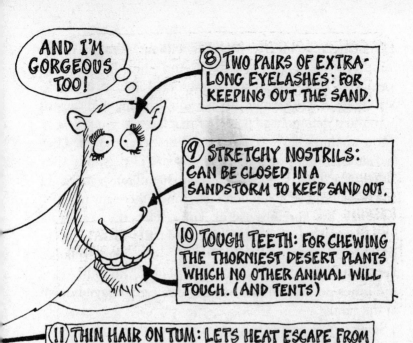

AND I'M GORGEOUS TOO!

⑧ TWO PAIRS OF EXTRA-LONG EYELASHES: FOR KEEPING OUT THE SAND.

⑨ STRETCHY NOSTRILS: CAN BE CLOSED IN A SANDSTORM TO KEEP SAND OUT.

⑩ TOUGH TEETH: FOR CHEWING THE THORNIEST DESERT PLANTS WHICH NO OTHER ANIMAL WILL TOUCH. (AND TENTS)

⑪ THIN HAIR ON TUM: LETS HEAT ESCAPE FROM THE CAMEL'S BODY TO COOL THE CAMEL DOWN.

Some hump-backed facts about camels

1 Can't tell one camel from another? Simple – just count their humps. A one-humped camel is called a dromedary. It lives in Arabia, Asia and Africa. Two-humped camels are Bactrians. They come from the Gobi. They get through the freezing winter by growing a shaggy, woolly coat.

I'M GLAD I REMEMBERED TO PUT MY COAT ON!

2 Camels can go for days and days without a drop to drink. But they work up a terrible thirst. And when they do get to water, they can guzzle down an awesome 130 litres in just 15 MINUTES! That would be like you drinking 400 cans of pop. You'd definitely go pop after that lot.

3 You wouldn't have recognized the first ever camels. They had short, stumpy legs and were the size of pigs. And they didn't have humps. They lived about 40 million years ago in North America (but you don't get camels there any more).

4 Camels are horribly useful. For a start, they can walk for miles without food or water. And carry loads of up to 100 kilograms (that's like you and two of your friends). Very handy for humping your tent about. And unlike cars and other desert vehicles, camels don't get bogged down in the sand.

5 Some desert people rely on camels for their living. They buy and sell them at camel markets (the white ones are worth the most). The more camels you have, the better off you are. Fewer than 20 is nothing to boast about. But 50 or more means you're rich. Camels also make brilliant wedding presents.

IT'S NOT ANOTHER TOASTER, IS IT?

6 And that's not all. People make tents and carpets from camel hair, and bags and rope from their hide. They even use camel pee to wash their hair. Apparently it leaves your hair nice and shiny and kills any irritating lice. Are you brave enough to give it a go?

7 Camel milk is crammed full of goodness and is rich in vital Vitamin C. (It's good for your teeth and bones. If you don't fancy a nice hot cup of camel milk before bedtime, you can also find it in fruit and veg.) You can either drink it straight, let it go off a bit or make it into yummy yoghurt. It tastes a bit like runny fudge. Fancy a spoonful?

FUDGE-FLAVOURED CAMEL YOGHURT RECIPE

Ingredients:
- some camel milk

Equipment:
- a large pan
- a bag made out of a goatskin
- a tripod made out of three sticks
- some rope

What you do:

1 Milk your camel. (Mind it doesn't kick you.)

2 Put the camel milk in the pan and heat it over the fire.

3 When it's warm but not boiling, pour it into the goatskin bag.

4 Hang the bag from the tripod, using the rope.

5 Give the bag a good shake. Repeat every few minutes for about two and a half hours until the mixture's thickened up a bit. (Warning: it will make your arm ache.)

6 Now tip it into bowls and serve it up to your friends. (If you dare…)

Horrible Health Warning
Camels aren't called "ships of the desert" for nothing. After an hour or two of sitting on a camel's back and swaying to and fro, you'll be feeling horribly seasick.

Desert plant dilemmas

Life's no picnic either for desert plants. Like animals, they need water to live. Without it, they'd shrivel up and die. In fact, they need water to make their food. Pretty vital, eh? Yet an amazing number of plucky plants live in the bone-dry desert. So how on Earth do they do it? It's a bloomin' miracle. Take the most famous desert plant of all, the skyscraping saguaro cactus...

WANTED

HAVE YOU SEEN THIS PLANT?

Name: SAGUARO CACTUS
Known haunts: Sonoran Desert, USA
Vital statistics: Height: 18 metres.
Weight: 10 tonnes. Age: up to 200 years.
Distinguishing features:

● Thick stem: for storing up to eight tonnes of water.

● Groovy pleats: lets stem double in size to fit all that water in.

● Waxy skin: to seal moisture in.

● Sharp spines: large leaves leak loads of water into the air. Fine spines lose much less. They also shade the cacti from the sun. And see off creatures who fancy a nibble.

● Roots: shallow and branching for sucking up as much rain as possible as soon as it hits the ground.

● Elf owl: nests in a hole inside the cactus. If it's an elf owl, it must be a saguaro. (Though it's not strictly a distinguishing feature.)

Any known accomplices: About 2,000 suspects, including the barrel cactus, teddy bear cactus, beavertail cactus, old man cactus, hedgehog cactus, organ pipe cactus, to name a few.

Any known enemies: Ruthless cacti rustlers who go around stealing cacti from the desert without getting a permit. They cart them off and sell them to budding gardeners. Stolen saguaros can fetch around US $1,200 (£750) for a cactus 5 metres tall, with an extra $50 (£30) bonus for each extra arm. In Arizona, there's now a full-time cactus cop to round up the rustlers.

Warning! This plant is armed and dangerous. A very prickly character indeed. Do not go near it. Even if you're dying for a drink. Especially if you're dying for a drink. Its juice is horribly poisonous to humans.

If you spot a cactus in the Sahara, something's gone horribly wrong. Cacti only grow in the USA. So it's either a mirage (see page 102) or you're in the wrong desert. Oops!

OOPS! I'M IN THE WRONG DESERT

Desperate desert fact file

NAME: Sonoran Desert

LOCATION: South-west USA and Mexico

SIZE: 310,000 sq km

TEMPERATURE: Hot summers from 41°C; cold winters to 3°C and below

RAINFALL: 50–250 mm a year

DESERT TYPE: High pressure

DESERT DATA:

• It's home to masses of wildlife, including pronghorn antelopes and mountain lions.

• It's prone to earthquakes because it lies close to the shaky San Andreas Fault, a colossal crack in the Earth.

• It's one of several North American deserts. You'll also find the Great Basin Desert, the Mojave Desert, the Painted Desert and the Chihuahuan Desert (yep, like those diddy dogs).

Bloomin' marvellous

Now, cacti may be the most famous plants in the desert but they're not the only ones. I've come across some marvellous bloomers on my travels. Here are some other ways in which these parched plants track down life-saving water. Ingenious, I think you'll agree.

One of the most down-to-earth desert plants is the marvellous mesquite bush. With roots an amazing 20 metres long, it can really get to the root of the problem. And the problem is finding water. Its roots reach down deep under the desert to suck up underground water. It's a bit like you slurping a drink through a 20-metre-long straw.

The cunning creosote bush does the opposite. Its tiny roots branch out far and wide to suck up dew and rain from all over the surface. Clever, eh?

The weird welwitschia of the Namib looks just like a giant turnip. At least, that's what it looked like to me. Except for the long, leathery leaves sticking out of the top. This peculiar plant only has two leaves but they can grow up to 3 metres long. They trail over the ground, getting terribly ragged and tattered at the edges. But they're also horribly helpful. They soak up fog blowing in off the sea and keep the wind-blown welwitschia well watered.

Last but not least, my own personal favourite. For most of the time, as you know, deserts look desperately dry and deserted. But in summer, when there's the best chance of some rain, it's a different story. Then the desert bursts into bloom. How? Well, there are billions of seeds buried under the ground. They've been there since the last time it rained, months or even years ago.

As soon as it rains, the seeds start to sprout. And in no time at all, the desert's decked out in fields of brilliantly coloured wildflowers, like desert daisies and dandelions. Now that's what I call bloomin' lovely.

But how on Earth do these flowers pick the best time to bloom? The truth is that these secretive seeds have a very special coating. It contains a chemical which stops the seeds sprouting until there's plenty of rain. Enough, in fact, to soak into the ground and wash the coating off. It's just as well. If the seeds tried to grow during a light shower, they'd soon wither and die when the sun came out again.

And finally...

Speaking of secretive, spare a thought for the desperate devil's hole pupfish. Its only home is a tiny underground pool in the middle of the desert. The rest of its habitat has all dried up. So the poor old pupfish has NOWHERE ELSE TO GO. Put yourself in the penned-in pupfish's place. Imagine being stuck in your geography classroom for ever. Now that's a horrible thought.

DESPERATE DESERT LIVING

Desert living may be cool for camels. But what about human beings? Surely the desert's too hot for them to handle? Well, incredibly it isn't. Despite the desperately harsh conditions, a mind-boggling 650 million people, that's 13 per cent of the world's population, live in the deadly deserts. And they've been doing it for years and years. They've found ways of coping with the heat and finding water that would put you to shame. But don't be fooled into thinking it's easy for them. Life in the desert can be horribly hard. Are you ready to find out how they do it? Why not spend a day with Sandy and the San people of the Kalahari Desert in Africa…

MY NOTEBOOK
A DAY IN THE LIFE OF THE SAN
by Sandy

Hi, Sandy here. I'm here in the Kalahari, spending the day with the San people. It's such an honour to be here, I can't tell you. These are people who really know how to survive in the desert. They'll certainly be able to teach me a thing or two.

Dawn
It's dawn and time to get up and make a fire. It's pretty chilly in the desert first thing in the morning. Lucky I brought a blanket. There aren't any bathrooms in the desert, of course,

but a bush makes a good toilet. There's no water either, at least not to waste, so instead of a wash, the San rub red sand over their bodies. Actually, it works quite well. Breakfast is a couple of spoonfuls of porridge.

dirty   clean

NOTES:

To make a fire the traditional San way, you need to use a fire drill. No, not the sort where you hear a loud bell and file out into the playground. It's made of two long sticks. One stick has a hole in it which the other stick slots into. Then you twist the long stick around in your hands until you get a spark. Simple when you've had plenty of practice!

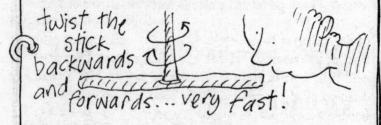

twist the stick backwards and forwards... very fast!

Early morning

After breakfast, the men set off hunting. They travel very light. All each hunter carries is a bag with his hunting spear, bow and arrows, digging stick (for finding water) and a fire drill (see Notes). I'm afraid I can't go with them this time but one of the hunters told me what happens. After walking for miles and miles through the desert, they finally track down an antelope. (There's some extraordinary wildlife in the Kalahari. Not just antelopes, but elephants and giraffes, too. It's finding them that's the tricky bit. Luckily, the San hunters know the desert like the back of their hands.)

bow

arrows

animal skin bag

When they track the antelope down, they fire. Their arrows are tipped with poison squeezed from a small but deadly beetle. The antelope doesn't stand a chance.

Back at the camp...

While the men are away, I'm off into the desert with the women and children to search for seeds and roots to eat. These are an important part of the San's daily diet. But it's hard work finding enough of them. I spend most of the time swigging water from my water bottle. The San women laugh at me. They don't need water bottles. When they're thirsty, they look for a small, dried-up plant sticking out of the sand. Goodness knows how they spot it. Looks just like a twig to me. Then it's time to start digging. It turns out that the twig thing actually belongs to a large, round tuber (a swollen plant stem). If you squeeze it, it drips with water. Very clever.

tuber

Any spare water is stored in empty ostrich egg shells which are sealed up and buried for later.

NOTES:
The San are experts at finding water. Here's how they make a traditional "sipwell":

1 They find a patch of damp ground and dig a deep hole.
2 Then they stick a hollow reed into the hole, like a drinking straw.
3 They fill the hole up, with the reed straw sticking out.
4 Gradually, water collects round the end of the straw.
5 When someone's thirsty, they simply slurp it up.

reed straw

SUCK UP water

Later that day
We get back to the camp just before the men. They arrive carrying the antelope. They have a really ingenious way of cooking it. First the men skin the antelope, then bury it in a hole in the hot sand. Then they light a fire in the hole and cover the whole thing with sand. When the meat's cooked, they cut it into strips. Brilliant. Then it's time for a feast! Everyone's hungry. Nothing goes to waste. Some of the meat is eaten straightaway. (And it's delicious, I must say.) Some is saved and

dried for winter. The antelope's skin is made into bags and clothes, and its bones are used for arrows. The San even eat the gristly bits in its ears. After all, it may be a while before they catch another one.

Sunset

After the feast, when we're all feeling full, the San sing songs and dance around the campfire until late into the night. They tell me that it's to thank the spirits for giving them a good day's hunting. Dances are also believed to help heal sick people. The San sing songs which remember their ancestors and ask the spirits for rain. It's a peaceful end to a long and tiring day. Now I'm really ready for my bed. I could sleep anywhere but I'm given a space on the ground behind a simple wall woven from dried grass. Each of the San has their own space. It's dry and out of the wind. Goodnight.

Next day
Up at dawn. It's time for the San to pack up their few belongings and set off for another campsite. They can't stay in one place for more than a few days. There's simply not enough food or water. And it's time for me to say goodbye.

I've had a brilliant time with the San. They're very kind and hospitable people, even though their lives are horribly hard. After even one day, I don't know how they keep going. I'll never complain about anything again.

NOTES:
The San have lived in the desert for 30,000 years. But now their lives are changing. Many have been badly treated and are being forced to leave their land. They're being made to settle down in shanty towns instead. It's a dreadful thing to happen to them. Some San are desperately fighting back to save their homes and their ancient culture. Otherwise they and their traditional desert skills may die out for ever. And that would be a terrible tragedy.

Teacher teaser

If you want to see your teacher really lost for words, forget Latin or ancient Greek. To confuse them utterly, speak Click. Start off with the word, "//kx'a". Helpful hint: to speak Click, it helps if you're good at pulling faces. Ready? First, pull your tongue quickly away from the sides of your mouth as if you're calling a horse. Then make a noise halfway between "k" and "g". Now make a little strangled sound as if you're choking. (Don't really choke.) Then finish off with an "aaahhh". Got all that? If you don't mind scaring yourself to death, try practising in a mirror.

But what are you trying to say?

Answer: Click is the language spoken by the San. In Click, "//kx'a" is the word for a type of tree. Click is horribly difficult to speak or understand, and can take years and years to master properly. And watch out. Even the tiniest little mistake can change a word's meaning utterly.

Desperate desert fact file

NAME: Kalahari Desert

LOCATION: Southern Africa

SIZE: 520,000,000 sq km

TEMPERATURE: Hot summers up to 49°C; cool winters with temperatures below freezing

RAINFALL: 130–460 mm

DESERT TYPE: High pressure and inland

DESERT DATA:

• It's mostly covered by ancient sand seas and dunes which formed over 10,000 years ago.

• It's home to the bizarre baobab tree which stores water in its trunk. When it's full it can measure 30 metres around its middle.

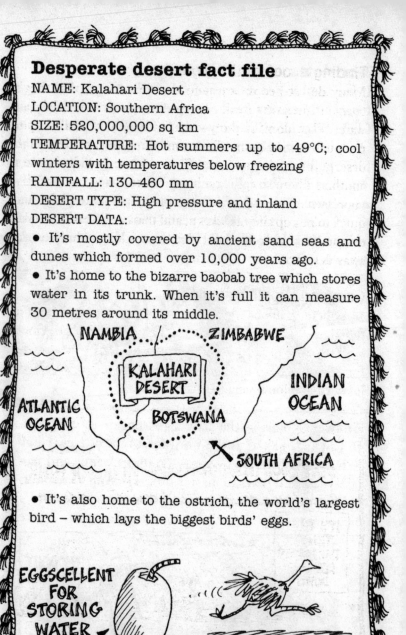

NAMBIA / ZIMBABWE

KALAHARI DESERT

ATLANTIC OCEAN

INDIAN OCEAN

BOTSWANA

SOUTH AFRICA

• It's also home to the ostrich, the world's largest bird – which lays the biggest birds' eggs.

EGGSCELLENT FOR STORING WATER

Finding a roof for the night

Many desert people are nomads. This means that they're constantly moving from place to place in search of food and water. They don't stay anywhere for long, just until supplies run out. Moving home all the time can get very tiring. In the desert, you can't just move from one ready-built house to another. There simply aren't any around. You have to carry your own home with you. So you need something that's quick to put up and take down, and that can be easily plonked on the back of your camel. Any ideas? What about a take-away desert tent?

Camping supplies catalogue

In a dilemma about which tent to choose? Don't worry. Our tents are specially designed to take the strain. Developed with the help of local desert people worldwide, they're ideal for camping out on the sand. We're proud to present our latest top-selling tent range...

① DESERT DE LUXE

STAY COOL IN A TRADITIONAL "HOUSE OF HAIR"

Based on a design passed down for centuries

IT'S THE TENT THAT WON'T LET YOU DOWN

MADE FROM THE FINEST CAMEL, SHEEP OR GOAT WOOL

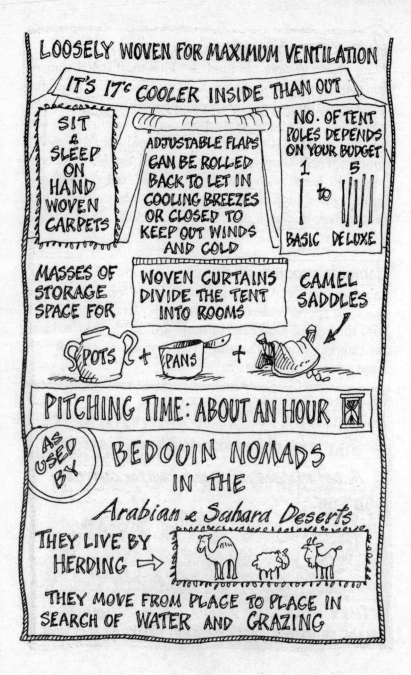

LOOSELY WOVEN FOR MAXIMUM VENTILATION

IT'S 17°C COOLER INSIDE THAN OUT

SIT & SLEEP ON HAND WOVEN CARPETS

ADJUSTABLE FLAPS CAN BE ROLLED BACK TO LET IN COOLING BREEZES OR CLOSED TO KEEP OUT WINDS AND COLD

NO. OF TENT POLES DEPENDS ON YOUR BUDGET

1 to 5

BASIC   DELUXE

MASSES OF STORAGE SPACE FOR

WOVEN CURTAINS DIVIDE THE TENT INTO ROOMS

CAMEL SADDLES

POTS + PANS +

PITCHING TIME: ABOUT AN HOUR

AS USED BY

BEDOUIN NOMADS IN THE

Arabian & Sahara Deserts

THEY LIVE BY HERDING ⇒

THEY MOVE FROM PLACE TO PLACE IN SEARCH OF WATER AND GRAZING

Two-Season Tents

TWO TRADITIONAL TENTS TO CHOOSE FROM. MADE FROM LOCALLY AVAILABLE MATERIALS. BOTH EASILY PACKED UP AND PORTABLE

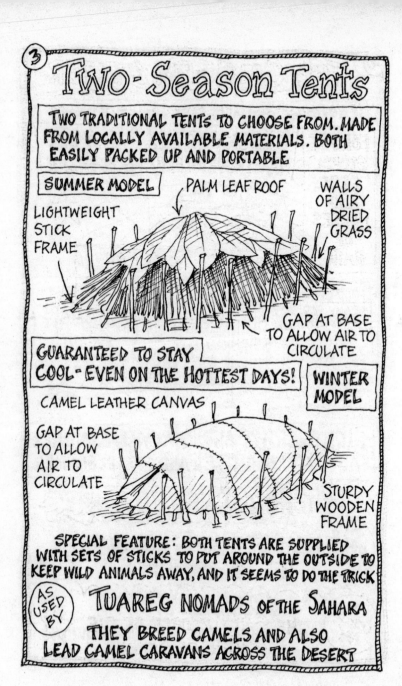

SUMMER MODEL

PALM LEAF ROOF

WALLS OF AIRY DRIED GRASS

LIGHTWEIGHT STICK FRAME

GAP AT BASE TO ALLOW AIR TO CIRCULATE

GUARANTEED TO STAY COOL - EVEN ON THE HOTTEST DAYS!

WINTER MODEL

CAMEL LEATHER CANVAS

GAP AT BASE TO ALLOW AIR TO CIRCULATE

STURDY WOODEN FRAME

SPECIAL FEATURE: BOTH TENTS ARE SUPPLIED WITH SETS OF STICKS TO PUT AROUND THE OUTSIDE TO KEEP WILD ANIMALS AWAY, AND IT SEEMS TO DO THE TRICK

AS USED BY **TUAREG NOMADS** OF THE **SAHARA**

THEY BREED CAMELS AND ALSO LEAD CAMEL CARAVANS ACROSS THE DESERT

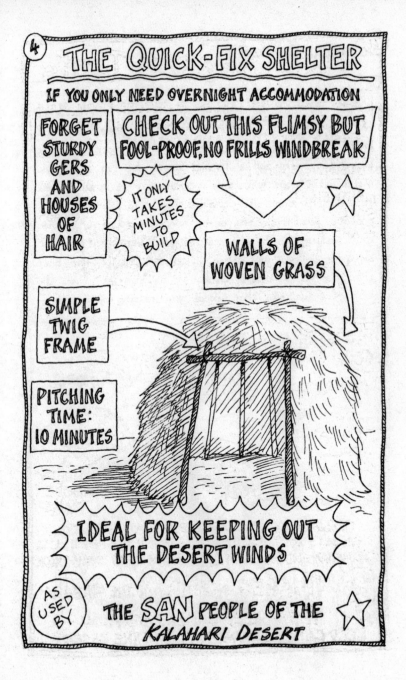

THE QUICK-FIX SHELTER

IF YOU ONLY NEED OVERNIGHT ACCOMMODATION

FORGET STURDY GERS AND HOUSES OF HAIR

CHECK OUT THIS FLIMSY BUT FOOL-PROOF, NO FRILLS WINDBREAK

IT ONLY TAKES MINUTES TO BUILD

WALLS OF WOVEN GRASS

SIMPLE TWIG FRAME

PITCHING TIME: 10 MINUTES

IDEAL FOR KEEPING OUT THE DESERT WINDS

AS USED BY THE SAN PEOPLE OF THE KALAHARI DESERT

Dressed for the desert

Sandy here again, with a word of warning. If you're heading off into the desperate desert, you need to dress for the part. So what's the latest in desert fashion? Well, for a start, practicality's more important than style. So shorts and a T-shirt won't do, I'm afraid, no matter how good you look in them. Forget looking cool. It's keeping cool that counts. You need clothes that'll protect you from the sand, wind and sun. Otherwise you'll end up burnt to a crisp and looking like a dried-up old prune. (And just how un-cool is that!) The best thing to do, I always think, is to look at what the locals are wearing. Then model your clothes on theirs:

The Tuareg certainly know how to dress. And how to stay cool as a cucumber. So what's the secret of their success?

VERY NICE

MODEL NO 1: TUAREG NOMAD
OUTFIT: TRADITIONAL DRESS
SCORE: 10/10 (AN OLD DESERT HAND)

TURBAN: WOUND AROUND HIS HEAD AND NECK TO STOP SUNBURN

LOOSE-FLOWING ROBES: NOT ONLY PROTECT HIM FROM THE SUN BUT ALLOW COOL AIR TO CIRCULATE INSIDE

BLUE VEIL: COVERS HIS FACE AND MOUTH TO KEEP OUT SAND, DUST AND EVIL SPIRITS. TUAREG VEILS ARE DYED DEEP BLUE. (AND ONLY MEN WEAR THEM.)

LONG COTTON ROBES: TO PROTECT HIS WHOLE BODY

LEATHER SANDALS: FOR WALKING ACROSS HOT SAND

I've modelled my outfit on the Tuareg's. After all, it works for them. Personally, I think it looks really cool.

MODEL NO 2: SANDY
OUTFIT: TRENDY EXPLORER
SCORE: 8/10 (NOT BAD, THOUGH I SAY IT MYSELF!)

SUN HAT: ESSENTIAL, WIDE-BRIMMED IS BEST

SUNGLASSES: TO PROTECT YOUR EYES FROM THE GLARE

SCARF: FOR COVERING YOUR MOUTH AND NECK

BLANKET OR JUMPER: FOR THOSE COLD DESERT NIGHTS

STURDY BOOTS: MIND YOUR FEET DON'T GET BURNT

SHOW OFF!

LOOSE, LONG-SLEEVED SHIRT AND LONG BAGGY TROUSERS: FOR COOLNESS, COTTON'S BEST

Here's an example of how not to dress for exploring the desperate desert. Don't geography teachers know anything?

MODEL NO 3: MR TOMPKINSON
OUTFIT: GEOGRAPHY TEACHER
SCORE: 3/10 (DESPERATE! A REAL
FASHION VICTIM.)

THINNING HAIR: WHERE'S THAT HAT?

TWEED JACKET: A BIT WORN AT THE ELBOWS

SHIRT AND TIE: FOR GETTING HOT UNDER THE COLLAR

BROWN, SUEDE SHOES: THAT HOLE WILL SOON BE LETTING IN SAND

Tea-time desert style

Now that you've got the clothes, it's time to meet the locals. Generally speaking, desert people are very hospitable. Even if they've never met you before, they'll offer you food and a place to stay. (Of course, once they get to know you better, it might be a different story!) So, it's important not to upset or offend them. (In the desert, you need all the friends you can get.) Here's a quick, step-by-step guide to minding your manners if a Tuareg invites you in for a cup of tea.

Are you brave enough to take tea with a Tuareg?

1 You arrive in a Tuareg camp. Act casual but be polite. Say "How do you do?" and shake hands with everyone, as if you've got all the time in the world. The Tuareg don't like to be hurried.

2 You're offered a glass of sweet mint tea. Drink it quickly and make lots of slurping noises. (This shows you're enjoying it.)

3 You're offered another glass of tea, then another. (By the way, it's very rude to refuse.) If it stops at three, congratulations. It means you're welcome to stay.

4 If you're given another glass (your fourth), you're welcome but not that welcome. Time to be on your way. Drink your tea, then get up, say your goodbyes (slowly, mind), and go.

Settling down

Not all desert people are nomads like the Tuareg. I mean, would you fancy moving house all the time? If you like the desert so much you can't bear to leave, why not pick a nice shady spot and settle down? You'll need water, of course, for drinking and growing your crops. But this is the desert so where can you find it? Well, the surface of the desert may look dusty and dry but there are buckets (and I mean buckets) of water under the sun-baked ground. You just need to know where to look for it.

Getting it out can be tricky, though. You could dig a well (you'll need to dig deep). Or you could sit and wait for the water to seep to the surface of its own accord and create a fabulously fertile … oasis. (You might be waiting for a very long time – it could take 10,000 years for the water to surface.) Here's the inside story of how a flourishing oasis is formed.

1 Rain falls on the ground (it may be miles away) and soaks into tiny holes in the rock. This is called an aquifer. It's like a giant, rocky sponge. (Not great for using in the bath.)

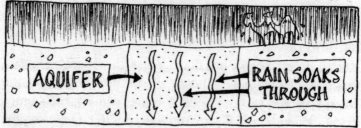

2 The water seeps along happily underground…

3 …until it comes to a split in the rocks and can't go any further. Then it's forced to the surface.

How green-fingered are you? With all that water lying around, you can grow loads of lovely fruit and veg. Like apricots, wheat and grapes, for a start. And palm trees... You might not think it to look at them but palm trees are horribly hardy and useful. You can eat their fruit (dates) raw, cooked or dried (like the ones you get at Christmas). You can use their trunks for building, their leaves for baskets and their seeds for camel food. And how about a tasty palm-bud salad? Delicious!

Horrible Health Warning

But before you get too comfy and settled, remember that the desert can play tricks on your eyes. Tricks that can drive you mad with thirst. Picture the scene. You've run out of water and you're desperate for a drink. Just then, you spot an oasis ahead of you. Phew! You're saved. You think. But however fast you walk towards it, it just gets further and further away. That's because the oasis doesn't really exist. It isn't actually there. It's a mirage. And it's maddening.

What happens is this:

1 A layer of warm air lies next to the ground.
2 It's trapped by a layer of cool air above it.
3 The layers bend the light coming from the sky.
4 So you think you see a refreshing pool of water rippling on the horizon. Lovely! But it's actually a reflection of the sky. (Worse still, it looks like it's fringed with shady palm trees. Sorry, more tricks of the light.)

Can you spot the difference?

Desperate desert survival quiz

Congratulations! You've come this far and you're still alive. You're really getting the hang of this desert-living lark. But what about your geography teacher? If he was stranded in the deserted desert, would he be able to survive? Or would his sense of adventure completely desert him? Try this deadly quiz on him to find out. All the answers are based on what local desert people would do in these situations. And they should know. After all, they've been surviving in the deadly desert since before your teacher was even born. And that's a very long time indeed!

1 You're in the Australian Desert and you're thirsty. Trouble is, there's no water for miles around. Just then, you hear a frog croaking. The sound seems to be coming from under the ground.

Do you bother to go and look for the frog? Yes/No

2 A diabolical dust storm is brewing in the Sahara Desert. You haven't got time to run for shelter so you decide to stand your ground and brave it out until the storm blows over.

Are you doing the right thing? Yes/No

3 You're in the Kalahari Desert with a group of San hunters. You're tracking an antelope when you spot a lion lurking in the bushes near by. You don't want to shout out a warning or the lion might hear you and charge.

San hunters have a range of hand signals to use in just this situation. Is this the right hand signal to use? Yes/No

4 You're looking for somewhere to pitch your tent and you spot a river valley (a *wadi*). It looks nice and level, and sheltered from the wind.

But is it really a safe place to camp? Yes/No

5 Your camel's playing up something rotten and you ask a local Bedouin camel herder for help. He tells you to pour spit down your camel's nose. But your camel's got a terrible temper and goodness knows what it'll do to you if you try.

Do you dare to follow the Bedouin's advice? Yes/No

6 The worst thing that could happen has happened. You've run out of water and you've still got miles and miles to go. You come across a Tuareg camp and stop to ask for supplies. You've learnt a bit of the local language and decide to try it out. Which word do you use for water? Would 'amise' do the trick? Yes/No

7 Oh dear, you're not having a very good day. You're out of suncream and your delicate skin is starting to burn. It'll be days before you reach a town where you can stock up on supplies. What can you use instead?

Would rubbing your skin with a watermelon work? Yes/No

Answers:

1 Yes. (Skip this next bit if you're squeamish.) This frog might save your life. It survives dry spells by storing water in its skin and sitting it out underground. Local Aborigines trick the frogs into croaking by stamping their feet on the ground. The stamping sounds to the frog like thunder which might mean rain!

Then the Aborigines dig the frogs up, hold them over their mouths and squeeeeeeeze!

2 No. The best thing to do in a dust or sandstorm is crouch down next to your camel and cover your face and mouth. That's where a Tuareg veil comes in handy. If you stand up and try to brave it out, you'll be blown away or end up having stinging sand kicked in your face. Painful.

3 No. That's the signal for a duck, silly. And ducks don't scare anybody. By the time you've realized your mistake, it could be too late. The lion will have had you for lunch. Here's the signal you should have used.

106

4 No. Learn a lesson from the locals and never pitch your tent in a *wadi*. Whatever you do. It might look very inviting at the moment but all that could change if it starts to rain. One minute, the *wadi*'s nice and dry, the next it's a raging torrent. Flash floods can happen at any time and the ground simply can't soak up the overflow. So it pours down the *wadi*. You won't have time to call for help. You'll already have been swept away.

5 Yes. Your camel's probably been plagued by evil spirits. And the ancient Bedouin cure for this is to pour a mixture of water and camel spit down its nose. It's guaranteed to turn your camel into … a … er pussycat. But mind your camel doesn't try to bite you. I mean, how would you like having spit poured down your nose?

6 No. You'll have to try again. In the Tuareg language "amise" means camel. The word for water is "aman". But make sure you've got something to give the Tuareg in return for the water. Never go empty-handed. Sugar cubes always go down well (for making Tuareg tea, of course).

7 Yes. Believe it or not, it will work nicely. Instead of suncream, the San crush up some roasted watermelon seeds and mash them into a pulp. It's brilliant at protecting their skin from the sun. Of course, it might also make you irresistible to insects, especially if they've got a sweet tooth…

Now add up your teacher's score…

He gets one point for each right answer. How did he do?

Score: 0-2. Oh dear! Your teacher's brain seems to have wilted in the heat. His common sense seems to have utterly deserted him.

Score: 3-5. Not bad! Your teacher has kept his wits about him and not got too bogged down in the sand. But that looks like a nasty camel bite. How on Earth did he get it?

Score: 6-7. Congratulations! Your teacher's survived! (Now don't all cheer at once!) Why not enter him in the next Mr Desert Competition? It's held every year in the Thar Desert, India. He'll need to do well in five categories: moustache-growing (the longer and curlier, the better),

turban-tying (against the clock),

public speaking (last year's winning speech was called "Why I like the desert so much", cringe),

camel-racing (over 500 metres) and, finally, camel fancy dress.

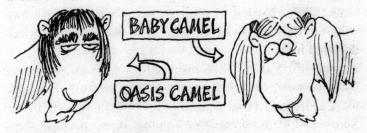

Do you think your teacher has got what it takes to win the Mr Desert crown?

So, armed with loads of local knowledge, you've packed your teacher off to the desperate desert and you're looking forward to a few days off. Don't worry, he'll be following in well-trodden footsteps. Not only have local people lived in deserts for centuries, hundreds of intrepid explorers have also set off to find out what all the fuss was about. Some have even lived to tell the tale. (Some have never been seen again.) For others, though, it was a case of out of the frying pan and into the fire. If you get my drift...

DARING DESERT JOURNEYS

People have been exploring the deserts for centuries. They've been blasted by sandstorms, bitten by camels and generally fried alive. Some have gone mad, or bad or lost their cool. Many have ended up lost. Dead lost. So why on Earth did they do it? Why put their lives at risk when they could have stayed in bed? Some of them were in it for the money. They wanted to open the desert up for trade. Others had no good reason for going. It just seemed like a good idea at the time. An adventure of a lifetime. They had no idea what lay in store. Some, like your teacher, studied how the local people coped and copied their age-old desert skills. Which greatly improved their chances of survival. Fancy a horrible holiday?

Horrible Holidays are proud to present their

SENSATIONAL SAHARAN SAFARI

Fed up with ordinary caravan holidays?

1,000 KM TO NOWHERE

Tired of squabbles about who gets the best bunk?

Had enough of sitting indoors in the rain?

BOOK YOUR PLACE TODAY

For a caravan holiday with a difference, book now on our deadly desert tour. (Better still, get your parents to pay.) Wave goodbye to crowded caravan sites, damp fields and traffic jams. Forget all about being squashed in a small space and those irritating cupboards that never stay shut. Time to get away from it all. Sleep under the stars in a luxury tent and soak up the age-old atmosphere of dreamy Timbuktu. It's the holiday that'll bring out the nomad in you.

Maximum 100 camels per caravan. (In the past, camel caravans travelling through the Sahara have been up to 1,800 strong).

HOW DO I SLEEP ON ONE OF THESE ?

Led by expert Tuareg guides. (They've been leading camel caravans across the Sahara for hundreds of years.)

Tried and tested transport. (Caravans have been used for centuries to carry people and goods across the Sahara. The goods included dates, salt and gold which were carried to market to trade. The people included local traders and intrepid explorers – remember René Caillié? – who came along for the ride.)

What one satisfied customer said:

"It was brilliant. I got on really well with my camel. It only bit me once or twice. I'll never go in an ordinary caravan ever again."

Small print: Our caravans are hand-picked for your comfort. But you won't find mod cons like hot showers, central heating or tellies on board. If you can't live without them, we suggest you try our brand-new Couch Potato Tour. Coming soon to a sofa near you.

Desperate desert fact file

NAME: Australian Desert

LOCATION: Australia

SIZE: 3,800,000 sq km

TEMPERATURE: Hot summers up to 53°C; cold winters down to –4°C

RAINFALL: Less than 100 mm a year

DESERT TYPE: High pressure; rain shadow

DESERT DATA:

• Two-thirds of Australia is desperate desert.

• This is made up of the Simpson, Great Sandy, Great Victoria and Tanami deserts.

• Uluru is a huge red rock worn away by the desert wind. It's sacred to the Aborigine people.

• The largest desert lake is Lake Eyre. It filled for the first time on record in 1950.

Crossing Australia, by camel

The Sahara is not the only desert where camels have come in handy. In 1860, two intrepid explorers, Robert O'Hara Burke and William John Wills, set off to cross Australia from south to north. It was one of the most daring expeditions ever. For years, people had wondered what lay in the middle of Australia. According to rumour it was either a great inland lake, or a huge, parched desert, bone-dry and baking hot. (In fact, the latter turned out to be true, as they would have known if they'd only bothered to ask the local Aborigine people who'd been living there for thousands of years. They knew every inch of the desert, and where to find precious food and water.) Anyway, just in case it was a desert, they took along some camels for the ride.

20 August 1860, Melbourne, Australia
When Burke and Wills set out from Melbourne on 20 August 1860, their camels were the talk of the town. The crowds who came to cheer the men on their way had never seen anything like them before. Some onlookers screamed. Others fainted. Others simply stood and stared. The camels had been brought over from India especially for this expedition and they were certainly causing a stir.

The expedition had taken months to plan. It was the largest and costliest ever seen in Australia. And it had already been a rocky road. Burke was brave and charming, it was true, but he was also horribly bad-tempered. He flew off the handle at anything.

(Secretly, it was said that bolshy Burke only applied for the job because he'd been unlucky in love. Or was it the large cash prize?) To make matters worse, Burke had no experience of exploration (he'd been a police officer before) nor of living in the bush. (And he wasn't the sort of man to think the locals could teach him anything.) Wills, on the other hand, was quietly spoken, loyal and dependable, and got on brilliantly with everyone.

Which was just as well. Just a few weeks into the trip, Burke sacked his deputy and gave the job to Wills.

There was no time to lose. They weren't the only ones making the journey. The great explorer, John McDouall Stuart, had already set out from Adelaide with a good few months' head start on them. But Burke had no intention of finishing second. No intention at all. So apart from being horribly high-handed and headstrong, he was also a man in a hurry. Did they make it? What did they find? Did Burke eventually swallow his pride and consult the local Aborigine people? Where better to look for the answers than in long-suffering Wills' expedition diary? (His real diary didn't go quite like this but it did give us most of the information we have about the jinxed journey.)

OFFICIAL EXPEDITION JOURNAL
by William John Wills

15 October 1860, Menindee
We're having a well-earned rest in Menindee. I'm already exhausted! The going's been rather slow, I'm afraid, since we set out from Melbourne. It looks like we've overdone the baggage (you name it, we've got it – food, guns, fishing tackle, camel shoes, tents, campbeds, books) so the wagons keep getting stuck in the mud.

115

(Not a desert in sight so far. The first part of the journey has taken us over muddy farmland through the pouring rain!) And those pesky camels keep frightening the horses.

Menindee's a tumbledown sort of place and Mr Burke doesn't want to hang around long. Can't say I blame him. Trouble is, summer's coming and it's already really too hot to carry on. Anyway, Mr Burke's decided that a group of us (Mr Burke, King, Brahe, Gray, Wright and myself) will press on with some of the camels and horses to Cooper Creek. The others will follow later with the rest of the supplies — we hope.

(Note: In Australia, the seasons are the other way round.)

me →

11 November 1860, Cooper Creek

I can't believe it. We've reached Cooper Creek at last. Thank goodness. Only 650 long, hard kilometres to get here. Wright's gone back to Menindee to fetch the others. The rest of us are too tired to do anything. Whoever warned us not to travel in summer was right — the heat has been terrible.

At first sight, this is a delightful spot, with a cool river and lots of pretty (and shady) eucalyptus trees. And even though we seem to have reached the edge of a desert, there are birds and fish everywhere — heaven! Or so we thought... But we've had to hang our supplies on strings in the trees. Why? Because otherwise the bloomin' rats will eat them. (I hate rats.) Oh, I forgot to mention – it's 43°C in the shade. I'm boiling. Will I ever get used to it? Now all we can do is wait for Mr Wright to return.

15 December 1860, Cooper Creek

Still here, I'm afraid. Wright's not back and Mr Burke is restless. That Stuart's really getting to him. So we (Mr Burke, King, Gray and me) are leaving tomorrow. We're making a dash for the Gulf of Carpentaria, the northernmost point of our journey.

I'm not looking forward to it. (Don't tell the others.) It's 2,400 kilometres there and back again, and guess what, we're walking all the way. I'm going to have blisters on my blisters! We're taking Mr Burke's horse and six of the camels, but not to carry us – worse luck. They'll carry the food (dried horsemeat) and water. We'll carry out our own guns and bedrolls. We're not taking tents. Apparently you don't need tents in the desert!

Mr B's told the others we'll be back in three months and to wait for us here. Lucky one of us is being optimistic.

our tents!

11 February 1861, the Gulf of Carpentaria (almost)

We've made it! It's been a dreadful journey and I can't believe I'm still here to write this diary. We walked and walked for 11 hours a day, every day, through blistering heat, thick swarms of flies and choking sandstorms. Real desert weather. (You can imagine how bad-tempered that made the camels.) All we had to eat were a few bits of that old dried horsemeat I mentioned and a handful of boiled plants. Apparently, they're called portulaca. Give me a nice juicy chop any day.

In January, the rains began and the ground turned into a mud bath. We travelled by night when it was a bit cooler — though it made it a bit difficult to see where we were going. Today, Mr Burke and I tried to reach the sea. It's only a few kilometres off. But wouldn't you know it — a pesky mangrove swamp forced us back. It was bitterly disappointing. Still, as Mr B says, at least we got further than that fool, Stuart (Mr B's words, not mine).

17 April 1861, Goodness knows where

What a rotten day! For days Gray's been complaining about feeling ill. But we all thought he was faking. (Anything to get out of carrying his own bed roll.) I mean, we're all exhausted and half-starved, not just him. So imagine our horror when we found him ... dead!

It took all day to bury him because we were so weak. The journey back from the coast has been a nightmare. It's rained non-stop since we left, and we've had to sleep out in the wet. (What was that about not needing tents?) We've run out of rations and our clothes are in rags. We managed to catch a snake to eat (and I'm afraid we had to eat four of the camels). But I don't know how long we can go on like this...

21 April 1861, Cooper Creek
I could have cried with joy when we arrived back at the camp this evening. But my happiness was short-lived. The others have gone. **GONE!** The camp's deserted. All that was left of them was a note pinned to a tree, showing us a place to dig. So we started digging, what else could we do?

Eventually, we unearthed a box with one month's rations inside and a scribbled note from Brahe. Would you believe it? They only left this morning. Just a few hours ago!

Brahe's heading back to Menindee. And who can blame him? He waited a whole four months for us to get back. But we're all too exhausted to go after him. We'll set out for Mount Hopeless tomorrow and try to reach the police station there. It seems like the only thing we can do.

27 June 1861, Cooper Creek

This is terrible. We can't go on for much longer. We've been going round in circles for days, getting nowhere. All our food and water is used up and there's only one camel left between us. (The other one got stuck in the mud so we shot it.) Things are looking pretty desperate now. Some friendly locals gave us some fish to eat — they have little enough to eat themselves.

But then they were on the way again. Can't say I blame them. If only we'd asked for their help before. Things might have been so different. I've written a letter to my father telling him what has happened. It might be my last. Unless we're rescued soon, we'll starve to death. . .

W.J. Wills

A very sad ending

If you're easily upset, skip this next bit or have your hanky handy. Two days later, Burke and King left the camp for the last time to look for help. Brave old Burke died on the way of starvation and exposure. When King got back to the camp, he found that Wills was also dead. King spent three months living with a group of Aborigines who took pity on him. When he was rescued, he was ragged, starving and half mad. Wills' (real) journal was found next to his skeleton.

It was a tragic ending. And it could all have been so different. If only heroic Burke and Wills had reached Cooper Creek just eight short hours earlier…

Desert exploration awards

To … sniff … cheer you up … sniff … a bit, the *Daily Globe* asked readers to vote for their top desert explorers. And here's Sandy to announce the results. Welcome to the Explorer Oscars.

MOST INTREPID EXPLORER (Male)

Runner-up

German geographer and explorer, Heinrich Barth (1821–1865) spent five years surviving in the Sahara. He spent six months living in Timbuktu, learning desert-craft from the locals. Heinrich was gone so long, he was given up for dead and his obituary was published in the paper. Then in August 1855, he emerged from the desert hale and hearty, with camel-loads of notes. Unfortunately he was so unpopular that no one really cared two hoots.

121

And the winner is…

In 1886, British soldier and explorer, Francis Younghusband (1863–1942), crossed the Gobi simply because it was there. All he took with him was a local guide, two porters, eight camels and a large supply of sherry.

What a guy! What's more he made it, covering 2,000 kilometres in 70 days. Was that it? Was it heck. After four days' rest, fearless Francis was off again, this time across the desperate Takla Makan. An outstanding performance.

MOST INTREPID EXPLORER (Female)
Runner-up

English explorer and writer, Gertrude Bell (1868–1926), comes second in this category. Frightfully posh Gertrude left behind a glittering social life in London and Europe to travel across the Arabian Desert. Of course, old habits die hard and even in the desert she always remembered her manners. She always dressed neatly in a nice dress and hat, and had the table laid with the best silver for dinner.

And the winners are…

Misses Mildred Cable, Eva French and Francesca French share this year's top award. A life of cream teas and croquet was not for these three plucky ladies. They spent years in China working as missionaries. Then, in 1926, they travelled across the Gobi Desert by mule-cart, accompanied by two saucepans, a cake tin, two jugs and a stove.

Only then did our heroines return to England, retire to a cottage in the country and write their book about the extraordinary places they'd seen and the people they'd met.

LUCKIEST TO BE ALIVE (In any category)
Runner-up

In 1894, Swede Sven Hedin (1865–1952) insisted on trying to cross the Taklan Makan, even though the local people warned him not to go.

He made it but he nearly died of thirst on the way. When his water ran out, with days of walking still to go, he survived by drinking chicken blood (he'd taken the chickens along for food). Later he gave a lecture in America about his murderous "March of Death". It made his audience so desperately thirsty they rushed out in droves for a drink!

And the winner is…

A unanimous decision. In 1844, Australian Charles Sturt (1795–1869), set off to explore the deserted middle of Australia. Unluckily for him, it was a desperately hot summer. So hot that all the waterholes dried up. Sturt got scurvy, almost went blind and could hardly walk. When he got home, two years later, his wife fainted when she opened the door. She'd given him up for dead.

Modern-day exploration

Feeling restless? Bored of sitting around at home? If all of this has given you a taste for adventure, why not set off to explore the desert for yourself?

I'M OFF TO EXPLORE THE SAHARA, MUM

ALL RIGHT, DEAR, REMEMBER YOUR TEA'S AT SIX

If camels aren't your cup of tea, there are lots of other ways of travelling. You can go by car, or truck or motorbike. Either way, you'll be in good company. Each year, 100 dare-devil drivers take part in the perilous Paris-Dakar Rally, straight across the scorching Sahara. The desert bit of the journey takes about three days. But don't expect to find nice straight roads and handy road signs to guide you over the sand dunes. You'll have to navigate by satellite. Even then, it's easy to take a wrong turn. Dead easy. Despite several trial runs and an official guidebook, many drivers still get horribly lost.

DESERT HOG!

And if that's not desperate enough for you, how about signing up for the strength-sapping Marathon des Sables. (If you want to know what that means, see what Sandy's got to say on the next page.) Be warned – this is seriously strenuous stuff. Not for the faint-hearted. Is it really that gruelling? Yes, it is. Have you ever tried to run in sand? It's impossible to get a firm grip with your feet so you're constantly slipping and sliding.

You have to run 225 kilometres over the sandy Sahara (in six stages). The good news is that you've got six days to do it in. The bad news is that you'll be running in temperatures of up to 58°C. You'll have to carry a 10-kilogram rucksack (that's like lugging around ten bags of sugar on your back) with your food, water and bed inside. And you'll need to wear shoes two sizes too big because your feet will swell up like balloons in the heat. (You'll also need to hold your nose when you take your shoes off. Phwoar!) Not to mention the blisters. Still keen?

That's French for Marathon of the Sands. But don't let that fool you. Just because it's got a fancy French name, it doesn't make it any less exhausting. And don't even think about cheating by getting a head start. You're only told the route the night before! Give me a camel any day!

WISE WORDS!

Earth-shattering fact
For the latest in desperate desert transport, you'll need to set your sights on outer space. The Lunar Rover was used by the American Apollo astronauts to explore the moon. But where was it tested? In the Californian desert, of course. It's the closest landscape to the moon we've got.

If you must head off into the desperate desert, always take some company. Never ever travel alone. There'll be no one to go for help if you run into trouble. A local guide is your best bet. Stick with them and you might just stand a chance. What? You've changed your mind about going? Well, I must say I'm glad. No point getting all hot and bothered for nothing. Why not have a well-earned rest and get to know the other side of the desert? The side that's horribly useful...

SPOILSPORT

DESERT TREASURE

What on Earth can you use a desperate desert for? You might think nothing at all. I mean, deserts are just a load of useless old rocks scattered about in the sand, aren't they? But looks can be deceptive. If you scratch the surface of the desert, you might get a surprise. Buried beneath the sand are some horribly useful desert spoils. It's just a case of knowing where to find them. Here are five things you might not expect to find in the desperate desert:

1 Life-saving salt. Salt isn't just tasty when it's sprinkled on chips, it can actually save your life. It's true! Believe it or not, your body needs some salt every day to stay alive. It keeps your body in working order. Normally, you get most of this salt from the food you eat. In the desperate desert heat, though, you lose spoonfuls of salt when you sweat. Luckily, there's plenty more around. Salt's been mined in the desert for thousands of years.

Here's what happens:

- A rare downpour of rain fills a dried-up lake.
- The water sucks up salt from the soil (desert soil's seriously salty).
- Then the water evaporates in the sun…
- … leaving a thick layer of life-saving salt.
- Miners use long poles to prise up huge slabs of salt. They cut the salty slabs into bricks.

- The bricks are sold to traders, loaded on camels and carried off across the desert …
- … to a special salt market. Here the salt's sold or swapped for tea, sugar or gold.

If this sounds too tiring, try a more restful remedy. Simply dissolve a salt tablet in a glass of water and slurp that down instead. (Drink it quickly – it tastes horrible!)

2 Oodles of oil. Oil is the most valuable desert spoil and there's barrels of the stuff under the desert. But how on Earth did it get there? Well, millions of years ago, the deserts were covered in swampy forests and seas.

When the plants and animals died, their bodies rotted and were buried under layers of rock. Which squashed them up into thick, gungy oil. Clever, eh? But you have to dig deep to get the oil out. Then it's pumped out of the ground and piped across the desert to an oil refinery. About a quarter of all the oil we use comes from the b-oil-ing Arabian Desert...

Desperate desert fact file

NAME: Arabian Desert

LOCATION: The Middle East

SIZE: 2,600,000 sq km

TEMPERATURE: Hot summers up to 54°C; cold winters down to –3°C

RAINFALL: Less than 100 mm

DESERT TYPE: High pressure

DESERT DATA:

• Oil was first struck in the 1930s. And it has made countries like Saudi Arabia seriously rich.

• Fierce winds called shamals blow twice a year whipping up tonnes of dust and sand.

• In 1950, temperatures fell to –12°C, with several centimetres of ice and snow. Brrr!

• Millions of Muslim pilgrims flock to the desert every year to visit the holy city of Mecca.

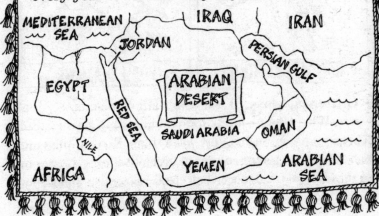

3 Dazzling diamonds. Diamonds in the desert? Sounds too good to be true? To see for yourself, head for the desperate Namib Desert. Hidden under its shifting sand dunes are dozens of dazzling diamonds. They formed tens of millions of years ago when the chemical carbon, in underground rocks, was heated to an incredibly high temperature by a volcanic eruption. Yes, things were very different in the desert tens of millions of years ago. Then the carbon cooled down and formed diamonds. Of course, diamonds don't look all posh and sparkly to start off with. (Well, would you if you were millions of years old?) They're buried under tonnes of gravel and dust. This is dug up and sent to a processing plant where all the gorgeous gemstones are sifted out. And it doesn't stop at diamonds. Gold (remember the story of gold–digging Pablo Valencia?), silver, opals, copper and iron are all to be found in deserts.

ROUGH DIAMOND   POSH DIAMOND

4 Glittering glass. If you can't afford diamonds, don't worry. What about a lovely lump of glittering glass instead? Just as pretty and won't cost you a thing. Parts of the sandy Sahara are covered in chunks of greeny-yellow glass. (Some of these chunks are soccer-ball sized.) Scientists think there may be 1,400 TONNES of the stuff scattered around the Sahara (so a tiny weeny lump shouldn't be missed). But where on Earth did all this glass come from? One theory is that, millions of years ago, a massive meteorite smashed into the Earth and melted tonnes and tonnes of sand. Then the sand cooled and turned into solid glass. Sounds reasonable!

5 Economy electricity. One thing you'll find plenty of in the desert is sunshine. The sun's in your face almost all day long. It's hot and it's also horribly useful. How? Well, at a solar power station, the sunlight falls on solar cells (like the ones you get in your solar-powered calculator) and is turned into electricity. It can be used to pump water from underground and heat water for people's homes. It's cheap, it's clean and it won't run out. And horrible geographers can't get enough of it! The largest solar-power station in the world is in the Mojave Desert in California.

Earth-shattering fact
If it's art you're after, head for the desert. The Nazca Desert in Peru. The ground is covered in patterns of lines and animal pictures, drawn about 5,000 years ago. (To get a good view, you'll need to stand on top of a hill. The pictures are enormous.) No one really knows why they're there. Some experts think they're a gigantic astrological chart, used for telling the future. Others claim they were runways for alien spacecraft. Weird.

How green is your desert?

The deserted desert's probably the last place you'd expect to find lush green fields. But farmers have been growing crops in the desert for thousands of years. So how do you turn bone-dry desert into fabulously fertile farmland? (The posh name for this is irrigation.) The answer is, you've guessed it, water! Buckets and buckets of water. And in the desert, it's easier said than done. If you were a desperate desert farmer, how would you water your fields? Decide which method you think works best, then check out the answers on pages 134–5. Here's Sandy to show you how it's done.

1 Dig a *qanat*. A *qanat* (kha-nat) is a man-made water tunnel dug deep under the ground. Here's how it works:

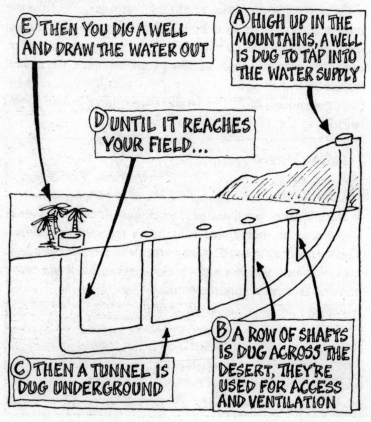

E) THEN YOU DIG A WELL AND DRAW THE WATER OUT

A) HIGH UP IN THE MOUNTAINS, A WELL IS DUG TO TAP INTO THE WATER SUPPLY

D) UNTIL IT REACHES YOUR FIELD...

C) THEN A TUNNEL IS DUG UNDERGROUND

B) A ROW OF SHAFTS IS DUG ACROSS THE DESERT, THEY'RE USED FOR ACCESS AND VENTILATION

2 Build a wall. Rain rarely falls in the Negev Desert in Israel. (Its name means "to dry".) So farmers have to make the most of even the diddiest downpour. They build low stone walls around their fields. The walls trap water which flows along channels into the fields.

3 Cover them with plastic. In the Negev again, you sometimes see fields full of plastic bags! It's true! No, you haven't gone mad. The bags are there to make sure your plants stay well watered.

4 Use a giant sprinkler. In the Sahara Desert in Libya, farmers water their fields with huge, spinning sprinklers. The sprinklers are fixed to long arms which move round the field like the hands on a clock. Tick, tock. They use water pumped from deep underground.

1 You'll be in good company if you choose this one. This really ingenious irrigation idea was first used by ancient Persian farmers 7,000 years ago. Want to know the best thing about it? Because the water flows underground, it doesn't evaporate and it stays ice cold. Cool, eh? In fact, qanats are so horribly clever they're still used today in Iran, the Middle East and China.

2 Another tried and tested method. The old ones are often the best, I always say. This one was first thought up 2,000 years ago. Recently it's been revived by farmers wanting to turn the desert green. And it's been such a bloomin' brilliant success that they've been able to grow peaches, almonds, wheat and tomatoes.

3 A simple but successful solution. Here's what you do. You lay a long pipe on the ground and plant your plants along them. Then you cover the whole thing in plastic. Let a steady trickle of water flow along the pipe to wet the plants at their roots. What's the plastic for? Well, it stops the water evaporating away in the sun.

4 A very good choice. Forget hose pipes and watering cans. Using these seriously sophisticated sprinklers, farmers have created huge wheatfields half a mile wide. They look like giant green saucers in the sand. The whole thing is controlled by computer.

So, which works best? Actually, they all do! And now that you've turned the dusty desert into farmland, here are some of the things you could grow…

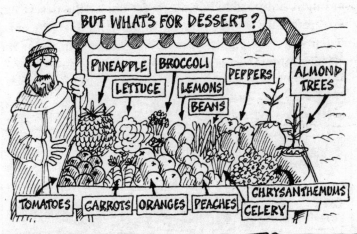

BUT WHAT'S FOR DESSERT?

PINEAPPLE BROCCOLI PEPPERS ALMOND TREES
LETTUCE LEMONS
BEANS

TOMATOES CARROTS ORANGES PEACHES CHRYSANTHEMUMS
CELERY

Earth-shattering fact
You know the saying "money doesn't grow on trees"? Well, money might not but plastic does. Honestly! And it's all down to a desert wildflower (OK so it's not exactly a tree) called popweed. Its oily sap can be turned into plastic for making things like toys, shoes and bits of cars. Might be worth planting a field or two?

Desperate desert cities

Fancy living in a place where the sun always shines, where there's loads of fresh air and wide, open spaces? Fancy living in the desperate desert?

You might not be able to wait to get out of the desert but there are plenty of others ready to move in. Take Phoenix, Arizona, for example. It's smack bang in the middle of the bone-dry Sonoran Desert.

Cities like it are springing up all over the desert especially in the USA and Australia. To keep a city like this going, you need about 76 BILLION gallons of water a year. That's an unbelievable number of buckets! So where does all this water come from? Some cities pump it from underground. Others bring it by pipe from far-off rivers.

SAND DUNE & CACTUS

ESTATE AGENTS

HELPING YOU GET AWAY FROM IT ALL

FOR SALE

House with large garden and swimming pool...

CALIFORNIA | NEVADA | UTAH

MEXICO

LOCATION: PHOENIX ARIZONA, USA
A PRIME DESERT SITE

SPECIAL FEATURES:
THE HOUSE COMES WITH AIR-CONDITIONING SO YOU CAN ENJOY THE WARMTH WITHOUT IT FRYING YOUR BRAIN. GREAT VIEWS OVER THE DESERT-ON A CLEAR DAY (AND IT'S ALWAYS A CLEAR DAY IN THE DESERT) YOU CAN SEE FOR MILES AND MILES

HAVE A NICE DAY, Y'ALL

SMALL PRINT
YOUR WATER SUPPLY COMES FROM THE COLORADO RIVER. IT'S BROUGHT BY PIPE STRAIGHT TO YOUR HOME.
SO MUCH WATER'S BEEN TAKEN FROM THE RIVER THAT IT'S RUNNING DRY.
EXPECT WATER SHORTAGES IN THE FUTURE.

Living in the desert has never been easier. But there's a horribly high price to pay. It's not just the rivers that are drying up. Horrible humans have been using up so much underground water, it could soon all be gone. Trouble is, some of it's been there for thousands of years. And it'll take thousands more to refill. So you could be waiting some time for a shower. Shame. And that's not all...

DESERTS IN DANGER

Using up all the water is one thing. But deserts are facing a deadlier danger – they seem to be on the move! All over the world, deserts are spreading. You might not think it's much of a problem. I mean, what difference would a bit more desert make? Well, it isn't a problem for the deserts. But for people living on the edge of some of the world's deserts, it can be a desperate situation. Turning a desert into fertile farmland is a horribly costly business. Many people have to scratch a living in fields at the desert edge. It's tough at the best of times. But if the desert grows and turns these fields into useless dust, they'll have nowhere to grow their crops. And no crops means no food. And that would be disastrous.

Deadly desertification

So why on Earth are deserts fraying at the edges? What's causing this deadly spread? Even horrible geographers can't agree. So we sent Sandy to try to dig up some answers…

"DESERT SPREAD" DOESN'T SOUND VERY POSH, DOES IT?

NOPE, IT DOESN'T. TECHNICALLY, HORRIBLE GEOGRAPHERS CALL WHAT'S HAPPENING DESERTIFICATION. IT'S BORING, I KNOW, BUT YOU GET THEIR DRIFT. THEY AGREE THAT IT MEANS HOW A DESERT IS MADE. SO FAR, SO GOOD. MIND YOU, THEY DISAGREE ABOUT ALMOST EVERYTHING ELSE.

I SEE. SO WHAT ACTUALLY HAPPENS THEN?

MOST GEOGRAPHERS THINK IT GOES SOMETHING LIKE THIS. ONE WAY OR ANOTHER, THE LAND AT THE EDGES OF THE DESERT TURNS TO DUST WHICH IS EASILY BLOWN AWAY BY THE WIND, OR WASHED AWAY BY RARE BURSTS OF RAINFALL.

CAN THIS HAPPEN NATURALLY?

YES, IT CAN. TINY CHANGES IN THE EARTH'S ORBIT AROUND THE SUN (THAT'S THE WAY THE EARTH TRAVELS AROUND THE SUN) CAN ALTER THE EARTH'S WEATHER. IF IT TURNS WINDIER AND DRIER THAN NORMAL, THERE'S TROUBLE AHEAD. THE LAND DRIES OUT AND TURNS TO DUST, AND YOU KNOW THE REST.

HAVE PEOPLE MADE MATTERS WORSE?

UNFORTUNATELY, THEY HAVE. USING THE SAME LAND OVER AND OVER AGAIN TO GROW CROPS DOESN'T GIVE IT ENOUGH TIME TO RECOVER. ALSO, TOO MANY SHEEP AND GOATS GOBBLE UP TOO MUCH GRASS, AND TOO MANY TREES ARE CHOPPED DOWN FOR FIREWOOD.

BUT HOW ON EARTH DOES THIS MAKE A DESERT?

WELL, THE CROPS SUCK UP GOODNESS FROM THE SOIL, LEAVING IT DRIED UP AND DEAD. YOU SEE? AND WITHOUT ANY PLANT ROOTS TO CEMENT THE SOIL TOGETHER, IT'S EASILY BLOWN AWAY. ALSO, ANY WATER WASHES STRAIGHT OFF THE SOIL INSTEAD OF SOAKING IN. WELCOME TO THE DESERT.

SO PEOPLE ARE REALLY TO BLAME, THEN?

YES AND NO. THE THING IS THAT PEOPLE HAVE TO GROW CROPS FOR FOOD, OR THEY'LL STARVE. BUT THE POPULATION'S GROWING SO FAST THAT THE LAND CAN'T TAKE THE PRESSURE. TROUBLE IS, IF THE LAND TURNS TO DESERT, PEOPLE WILL STARVE ANYWAY. IT'S A VERY VICIOUS CIRCLE.

HOW MUCH NEW DESERT ARE WE TALKING ABOUT?

SOME GEOGRAPHERS THINK THAT ABOUT 100 SQ KM OF LAND IS TURNING TO DUST EVERY DAY! (THAT'S ABOUT THE SAME AS TEN FULL-SIZED SOCCER PITCHES.) SPELLING DISASTER FOR ABOUT 900 MILLION PEOPLE. THAT'S ABOUT A SIXTH OF THE WORLD'S POPULATION.

BLIMEY. AND WHICH PLACES ARE MOST AT RISK?

IT'S A WORLDWIDE PROBLEM, I'M AFRAID. BUT PARTS OF AFRICA ARE PARTICULARLY AT RISK. ESPECIALLY A REGION CALLED THE SAHEL ON THE SOUTHERN EDGE OF THE SAHARA. IN THIS CASE, HUMAN ACTIVITY AND NATURAL CAUSES TRIGGERED OFF A MASSIVE TRAGEDY.

The Sahel, Africa, 1984-1985

In 1984-1985, the Sahel suffered one of the worst droughts ever to strike Africa. Very little rain falls in this part of the world normally. But this year, the rains completely failed. With no water, the land quickly turned to dust. The local farmers watched helplessly as their precious crops withered and died.

There was nothing they could do. But worse was to come. Without any food to eat, people began to starve to death. In the dreadful famine that followed, almost a million people died of hunger and disease. In Ethiopia alone, about half the country's cattle starved to death. All over the region, desperate villagers left their homes and farms in search of food and water. Millions ended up sheltering in refugee camps and feeding centres set up to help the victims. Some had walked for days. They were homeless, hungry and terrified. Worst of all, no one knew how long their nightmare would last.

The word Sahel means shore. But not the sort of shore you'd find by the sea. It describes the strip of land along the southern edge of the vast Sahara Desert. The Sahel stretches for 500 kilometres from Senegal and Mauritania on the west coast, to Sudan and Ethiopia in the east, and covers about a fifth of Africa.

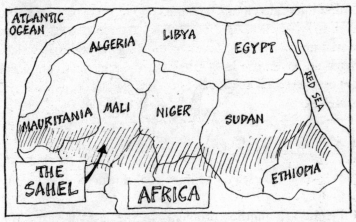

For eight months of the year, between October and June, the Sahel is bone dry. But there are a few rainy months between June and September. During this time, enough rain usually falls for farmers to grow their crops and raise their animals. Usually. But not this time. This time there was no rain. And it caused a catastrophe. And it wasn't the first time. Devastating droughts had already struck the Sahel in the 1960s and 1970s.

So why on Earth did this terrible tragedy happen?

- Put simply, drought means a lack of rainfall which can last for months or even years. It's the usual state of things in the desert. The problems start if a drought comes unexpectedly or lasts longer than usual. Then it can be disastrous.

- The Sahel has suffered droughts on and off for the last 40 years. So what on Earth makes it so drought-prone? Some geographers blame the Atlantic Ocean (off the western end of the Sahel). But how can a sea possibly be to blame? It's all down to temperature. If the sea is cooler than normal, less moisture rises from it into the air, so you don't get rain clouds forming.

Why does the sea sometimes cool down? Nobody really knows.

- People are another problem. In the last 50 years, the Sahel's population has grown very quickly, thanks to a few years of really heavy rain. With more mouths to feed, farmers had to grow more crops more quickly. Which put the land under pressure. It never had time to recover. In the past, it was left for 15–20 years before being farmed again. Now it was used within five years.

- And it doesn't stop there. We use technology to make life easier, but in the Sahel it made things worse. New equipment meant people could dig deeper wells. Which meant they could keep more animals. Which ate all the plants, so the soil dried up and, well, you know the rest. In the Sahel, staying alive is a horribly delicate balance.

• When the land turns to dust and blows away, where on Earth does it go? Into the awesome atmosphere, of course.

Where it too can actually reduce the chances of rain. How? Well, a thick, choking dollop of dust stops the air moving so it can't cool and condense into clouds. So even the dust stirred up during a drought adds to the problem. Pretty desperate, really.

Horrible Health Warning

And it's not just deserts that are drying up. The Aral Sea is, too. (Actually it isn't a real sea. It's a salty inland lake. It's just called a sea. See?) The arid Aral lies in the middle of the Turkestan Desert (see page 148). And for the past 14,000 years, it has relied on two large rivers to fill it with water. But not any more. Now so much water has been piped from the rivers for irrigation and drinking that the Aral Sea is shrinking. Between 1960 and 1990 it halved in size. And it's still getting smaller. What water's left is now so salty that fish can't survive. And once-busy fishing ports are now left stranded on the shore, miles away from the water.

Desperate desert fact file

NAME: Turkestan Desert

LOCATION: Central Asia

SIZE: 450,000 sq km

TEMPERATURE: Hot summers up to 49°C. Freezing winters down to −42°C

RAINFALL: 70–150 mm

DESERT TYPE: Inland desert

DESERT DATA:

• It's two deserts really – the Kara Kum (Black Sands) and the Kyzyl Kum (Red Sands).

• It's dotted with bare patches of clay called takyrs which are used for collecting water. This means farmers can grow exotic fruit like melons and grapes in the middle of the desert.

• Ninety per cent of the Kara Kum is crisscrossed by greyish-coloured sand dunes, which are hundreds of kilometres long.

• Thirty million years ago, the whole desert was covered in salty sea.

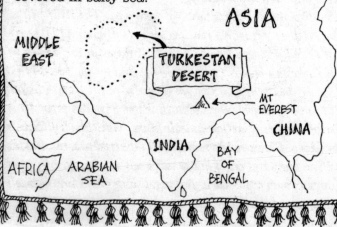

Stopping the spread

Deserts are horribly sensitive. One false move, and before you know it, you've got a full-blown desert disaster on your hands. But is it all doom and gloom? Are the deserts really taking over? What's being done to hold them back? The good news is that people are trying their best to stop the rot. Desert people all over the world are working hard to strand the sand. But it's a horribly tricky, costly business and many desert countries are very poor. They don't have enough money to spend on food let alone on diverting the deserts. It's a desperate dilemma. Here are just a few of the things they're testing out:

1 Planting trees. The tree roots stick into the soil and stop it blowing away so fast. Tough grasses are good for this, too. Besides, the trees also act like windbreaks to slow down the blasting wind. Over the last ten years in Ethiopia, people have planted 500 million hardy eucalyptus and acacia trees. That's an awful lot of digging.

WHEN I SAID LET'S PLANT A TREE, I MEANT OUTSIDE!

2 Soil-stopping stones. In Africa, farmers lay lines of stones across their fields. These stop the rain simply washing away the soil. It's simple but brilliant. In just a few years, farmers can double their harvests and put some grain in store in case drought strikes again.

3 A load of old dung. Here's another age-old way local people have of turning the desert green again. Why not try it for yourself?

What you need:
- Some cow poo
- A spade
- Some grass seeds
- A clothes peg

What you do:

a) Dig a semi-circular hole in the ground. (It seems that this is the shape that works best. But you don't need to be too picky.)

b) Then fill it with the cow poo. (This is where the peg comes in handy.)

c) Sprinkle the seeds on to the poo.

d) Wait for a few months. (You'll soon get used to the smell.)

What you'll see:
Water condenses on to the nice, warm poo and makes the grass seeds sprout. Soon the sand's covered in lush, green grass. Which, by the way, is brilliant for feeding to your cows! (Then just wait a few hours, grab your spade and off you go again.) Don't forget to remove the clothes peg.

4 What's the mat-ter? In the Gobi Desert, people scatter straw mats over the sand dunes to stop them creeping forward. The mats are spread out like the squares on a chess board. They break up the wind's flow which makes it much weaker so it doesn't have enough strength left to shift the sand.

5 An oily option. In Saudi Arabia, shifting sand dunes bury farms and villages, and clog up vital oil pipelines. But what on Earth can be done? One method is to spray the sand with oil (once you've got the pipeline unclogged, of course). It's quick, cheap and it seals the sand and stops it moving. Sounds the perfect solution? There's just one problem. Unfortunately, the oil also kills off precious trees and plants. And that's the last thing you need. Do any especially tough plants survive? Well, there's one...

Earth-shattering fact
If real trees don't work, try planting some plastic palm trees. Yep, plastic. They look just like the real thing but they don't need watering which is very good news. So how on Earth can you beat back the desert with some plastic plants? The theory is that the trees trap moisture in their leaves and stems at night, then slowly release it during the day. In a few years' time, this will cool down the climate so (real) rain clouds can form. Will it work? Nobody has the faintest idea.

HMM, INTERESTING NEW FLAVOUR

CRUNCH!

MUNCH!

A SANDY FUTURE?

So are the deserts really moving? Or is it just another mind-boggling mirage? Here's what the experts have to say. Don't expect the answers to be quick or simple. Horrible geographers hardly ever see eye to eye. Take these two, for instance. They're keeping their heads firmly stuck in the sand. So it's up to you to make your own mind up.

It's all true, the deserts are getting bigger. And things can only get worse. Already, the Sahara's shifting forward by about 6 whole kilometres a year. At this rate, it'll spread right across the Mediterranean and into Spain, Greece and Italy. (Perhaps the Romans were right after all.) And before you know it, you'll have a sand dune knocking at your door... I'm outta here!

I CAN'T STAND EXPERTS

See what I mean? Desperate, isn't it? And it doesn't stop there. Other experts claim that the Sahara Desert isn't growing at all. Actually, they say, it's shrinking! And they've got the photographs (snapped by satellite cameras) as proof.

So there. Confused? It's baffling enough to bake your brains. But that's geography for you. Nothing's ever cut and dried. You never know what's around the next corner, let alone around the next desert. And that's what makes it so horribly exciting.

HORRIBLE INDEX

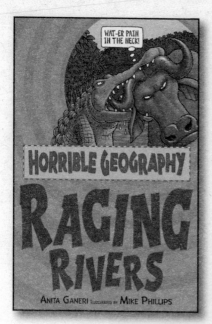

THEY'RE IN THE SHOPS NOW!